ÆSOP'S FABLES.

Wisdom can make our lives happier, and the world a better place for all.

Susie Moore

THREE HUNDRED

ÆSOP'S FABLES

LITERALLY TRANSLATED FROM THE GREEK

BY THE

REV. GEO. FYLER TOWNSEND, M.A.

With Fifty Illustrations by Harrison Weir

REVISED EDITION BY SUSIE MOORE

AESOP CLASSICS

Oxford, UK

First published by

GEORGE ROUTLEDGE AND SONS

BROADWAY, LUDGATE HILL, LONDON

GLASGOW AND NEW YORK

AESOP Classics
An imprint of AESOP Publications
28 Abberbury Road, Oxford OX4 4ES, UK
www.aesopbooks.com

Aesop's Fables is in the public domain.

This book is a facsimile of an edition
translated by the Rev. George Fyler Townsend,
illustrated by Harrison Weir and published by
George Routledge and Sons in 1880.

A catalogue record of this book is
available from the British Library.

Condition of sale:

ISBN: 978-1983741883

*Dedicated to all of us
who are greedy for
wisdom and beauty*

INTRODUCTION

I always thought it was a crime when people didn't use their unique gifts within their lifetime – their ability to sing, teach, lead, write, build things. Whatever you were born with, you must use it. I used to consider it almost stealing – holding back from the world the talent, skills and strengths that are still inside you.

Nothing nails this emotion more than Aesop's fable of The Miser and the Gold:

> Once upon a time there was a Miser who used to hide his gold at the foot of a small tree in his garden; but every week he used to go and dig it up and gloat over his gains. A robber, who had noticed this, went and dug up the gold and stole it. When the Miser next came to gloat over his treasures, he found nothing but the empty hole. He tore his hair, and raised such an outcry that all the neighbours came around him, and he told them how he used to come and visit his gold. "Did you ever take any of it out?" asked one of them.
>
> "Nay," said he. "I only came to look at it."
>
> "Then come again and look at the hole," said a neighbour; 'it will do you just as much good."
>
> *Wealth unused might as well not exist.*

That's what Aesop's Fables are: Wealth, Truth, Wisdom. It's the quality of having experience, knowledge and good judgement. The value of being wise.

Reading and learning Aesop's Fables from a young age imparted knowledge in me that I have used throughout the years for strength, guidance and comfort. They are a beautifully designed rare collection of gems, illustrated in this edition by the superb artist Harrison Weir, entertaining and enlightening anyone from the age of five to eighty-five.

You probably know some of them already:

The story of the hare and the tortoise: *slow and steady wins the race*.

The warning about the boy who cried wolf: *a liar will not be believed when he tells the truth*.

The fox and his sour grapes: *it's easy to despise what you cannot get*.

Very little is known about the legendary ancient Greek writer whose stories of clever animals and foolish humans are considered to be Western civilization's first morality tales. According to Heredotus, Aesop was a slave who lived in Samoa in the sixth century BC and who eventually earned his freedom through his storytelling and went on to serve as advisor to a king.

Abraham Lincoln used to employ Aesop's fables when illustrating a point. He would open his argument by saying, 'This reminds me of a story about…'

Storytelling is ageless and Wisdom is the greatest gold. It is my dream for a copy of Aesop's Fables to be in every home: it is as vital as bread and butter. The best way to share, learn and teach is through stories.

The Fables can be opened on any page. There is no plot to remember. Every story is complete, fresh, clear – and sometimes hilarious.

Like the story of the miser and the gold, my Polish grandfather had an expression: "Spend some, save some, share some with others who need it." Out of love and respect for Aesop and his timeless collection, a donation from the sale of every copy of this book will be a given to children's charities.

With love and best wishes,

Susie Moore

PREFACE

THE Tale, the Parable and the Fable are common and popular ways of conveying instructions. Each is distinguished by its own characteristic. The Fable contains a short but real narrative and seeks to convey a hidden meaning, not so much by the use of language but by introduction of fictitious characters: the animals of the field, the birds of the air the trees of wood or the beasts of the forest. The Fox is always cunning, the Hare timid, the Lion bold, the Wolf cruel, the Bull strong, the Horse proud and the Ass patient. They all speak human language, which leads to a particular moral lesson. The Fable is about moral maxim, social duty, political truth, and what is pure, honourable and praiseworthy.

The history of fables is long and rich. Some of the fables had, no doubt, in the first instance, a private and primary interpretation. They referred to some passing event or to some individual acts of wrongdoing, designed to meet special circumstances.. Fables are so admirably constructed as to be fraught with lessons of general utility and of universal application. Originally told from person to person as much for entertainment purposes, but largely as a means of relaying or teaching a moral lesson.

For example a fable "Frog Asking for a King" was spoken by Æsop for the immediate purpose of reconciling the inhabitants of Samos and Athens to their respective rulers, Periander and Pisistratus.

The collection of these Fables was printed as early as 1475–80. Reintroducing Æsop's Fables to a place in the literature of the world came about in the early part of the seventeenth century. An edition of these fables was printed in 1610; it was a noble effort to honour the great fabulist and was the most perfect collection of Æsop's Fables ever yet published.

No book, with the exception of the Holy Scriptures, has had a wider circulation than Æsop's Fables. They have been translated into a great number of languages, both European and Oriental, and have been read – and will be read – for generations, alike by Jews, Christians, Muslims, Hindus, Buddhists and atheists.

The publishers of this edition have sought to give as nearly a literal translation as possible of the Greek text. They hope that if readers should miss the smoothness and thoroughly English tone, they will be more than repaid by gaining a nearer approach to the spirit, thoughts, and (in some cases) to the epigrammatic terseness of the original.

SOME of the fables in this edition are obtained from ancient authors prior to the time in which Æsop lived. Some of them can also be traced to the Monks of the Middle Ages. This collection rightfully bears his name, because he composed a large number of them to secure himself the right to be considered the father of Greek fables, the founder of this class of writing, and to occupy the position of the first moralist.

The publishers of this edition played a a big role in increasing the circle of admirers of Æsop's Fables and in promoting a wider acquaintance with fables, the wisdom, excellence and suitability to every condition of humanity.

Fables use household words in the daily conversation of the inhabitants of all countries and this edition of the Fables is intended both to amuse the young and to instruct the thoughtful. It is well suited to teach all who study them those lessons useful for their guidance in every position of social, political, civil or domestic life.

The Reverend G. F. Townsend (1814–1900) was the translator of the standard English edition of Æsop's Fables.

Harrison Weir, artist, author, journalist (1824–1906) designed all of the illustrations for the 300 fables in this edition.

Susie Moore (1984–) wrote the Introduction and sponsored the reprinting and restoration of this classic edition of Æsop's Fables.

LIFE OF ÆSOP.

———◇———

THE Life and History of Æsop is involved, like that of Homer, the most famous of Greek poets, in much obscurity. Sardis, the capital of Lydia; Samos, a Greek island; Mesembria, an ancient colony in Thrace; and Cotiæum, the chief city of a province of Phrygia, contend for the distinction of being the birthplace of Æsop. Although the honour thus claimed cannot be definitely assigned to any one of these places, yet there are a few incidents now generally accepted by scholars as established facts, relating to the birth, life, and death of Æsop. He is, by an almost universal consent, allowed to have been born about the year 620 B.C., and to have been by birth a slave. He was owned by two masters in succession, both inhabitants of Samos, Xanthus and Jadmon, the latter of whom gave him his liberty as a reward for his learning and wit. One of the privileges of a freedman in the ancient republics of Greece, was the permission to take an active interest in public affairs; and Æsop, like the philosophers Phædo, Menippus, and Epictetus, in later times, raised himself from the indignity of a servile condition to a position of high renown. In his desire alike to instruct and to be instructed, he travelled through many countries, and among others came to Sardis, the capital of the famous king of Lydia, the great patron, in that day, of learning and of learned men. He met at the court of Crœsus with Solon, Thales, and other sages, and is related so to have pleased his royal master by the part he took in the conversations held with these philosophers, that he applied to him an expression which has since passed into a proverb, "μᾶλλον ὁ Φρύξ." "The Phrygian has spoken better than all."

On the invitation of Crœsus he fixed his residence at Sardis, and was employed by that monarch in various difficult and delicate affairs of State. In his discharge of these commissions he visited the different petty republics of Greece. At one time he is found in Corinth, and at another in Athens, endeavouring, by the narration of some of his wise fables, to reconcile the inhabitants of those cities to the administration of their respective rulers, Periander and Pisistratus. One of these ambassadorial missions, undertaken at the command of Crœsus, was the occasion of his death. Having been sent to Delphi with a large sum of gold for distribution among the citizens, he was so provoked at their covetousness that he refused to divide the money, and sent it back to his master. The Delphians, enraged at this treatment, accused him of impiety, and, in spite of his sacred character as ambassador, executed him as a public criminal. This cruel death of Æsop was not unavenged.

The citizens of Delphi were visited with a series of calamities, until they made a public reparation of their crime; and "the blood of Æsop" became a well-known adage, bearing witness to the truth that deeds of wrong would not pass unpunished. Neither did the great fabulist lack posthumous honours; for a statue was erected to his memory at Athens, the work of Lysippus, one of the most famous of Greek sculptors. Phædrus thus immortalizes the event :—

> Æsopo ingentem statuam posuere Attici,
> Servumque collocarunt æternâ in basi :
> Patere honoris scirent ut cuncti viam ;
> Nec generi tribui sed virtuti gloriam.

These few facts are all that can be relied on with any degree of certainty, in reference to the birth, life, and death of Æsop. They were first brought to light, after a patient search and diligent perusal of ancient authors, by a Frenchman, M. Claude Gaspard Bachet de Mezeriac, who declined the honour of being tutor to Louis XIII. of France from his desire to devote himself exclusively to literature. He published his Life of Æsop, Anno Domini 1632. The later investigations of a host of English and German scholars have added very little to the facts given by M. Mezeriac. The substantial truth of his statements has been confirmed by later criticism and inquiry. It remains to state that, prior to this publication of M. Mezeriac, the life of Æsop was from the pen of Maximus Planudes, a monk of Constantinople, who was sent on an embassy to Venice by the Byzantine Emperor Andronicus the elder, and who wrote in the early part of the fourteenth century. His life was prefixed to all the early editions of these fables, and was republished as late as 1727 by Archdeacon Croxall as the introduction to his edition ot Æsop. This life by Planudes contains, however, so small an amount of truth, and is so full of absurd pictures of the grotesque deformity of Æsop, of wondrous apocryphal stories, of lying legends, and gross anachronisms, that it is now universally condemned as false, puerile, and unauthentic. It is given up in the present day, by general consent, as unworthy of the slightest credit.

LIST OF ILLUSTRATIONS.

FABLES OF ÆSOP.

THE LION AND THE MOUSE.

A LION was awakened from sleep by a Mouse running over his face. Rising up in anger, he caught him and was about to kill him, when the Mouse piteously entreated, saying: "If you would only spare my life, I would be sure to repay your kindness." The Lion laughed and let him go. It happened shortly after this that the Lion was caught by some hunters, who bound

him by strong ropes to the ground. The Mouse, recognizing his roar, came up, and gnawed the rope with
his teeth, and setting him free, exclaimed : " You ridiculed the idea of my ever being able to help you, not
expecting to receive from me any repayment of your
favour ; but now you know that it is possible for even a
Mouse to confer benefits on a Lion.

THE WOLF AND THE LAMB.

A Wolf meeting with a Lamb astray from the fold,
resolved not to lay violent hands on him, but to find
some plea, which should justify to the Lamb himself his
right to eat him.   He thus addressed him : " Sirrah, last
year you grossly insulted me."   " Indeed," bleated the
Lamb in a mournful tone of voice, " I was not then
born."   Then said the Wolf, " You feed in my pasture."
" No, good sir," replied the Lamb, " I have not yet
tasted grass."   Again said the Wolf, " You drink of my
well."   " No," exclaimed the Lamb, " I never yet drank
water, for as yet my mother's milk is both food and
drink to me."   On which the Wolf seized him, and ate
him up, saying, " Well ! I won't remain supperless, even
though you refute every one of my imputations."

The tyrant will always find a pretext for his tyranny.

THE ASS AND THE GRASSHOPPER.

An Ass having heard some Grasshoppers chirping, was
highly enchanted ; and, desiring to possess the same
charms of melody, demanded what sort of food they
lived on, to give them such beautiful voices.   They
replied, " The dew."   The Ass resolved that he would
only live upon dew, and in a short time died of hunger.

THE WOLF AND THE CRANE.

A Wolf, having a bone stuck in his throat, hired a Crane, for a large sum, to put her head into his throat, and draw out the bone. When the Crane had extracted the bone, and demanded the promised payment, the Wolf, grinning and grinding his teeth, exclaimed: " Why, you have surely already a sufficient recompense, in having been permitted to draw out your head in safety from the mouth and jaws of a wolf."

In serving the wicked, expect no reward, and be thankful if you escape injury for your pains.

THE FATHER AND HIS SONS.

A FATHER had a family of sons who were perpetually quarrelling among themselves. When he failed to heal their disputes by his exhortations, he determined to give them a practical illustration of the evils of disunion; and for this purpose he one day told them to bring him a bundle of sticks. When they had done so, he placed the faggot into the hands of each of them in succession, and ordered them to break it in pieces. They each tried with all their strength, and were not able to do it. He next unclosed the faggot, and took the sticks separately, one by one, and again put them into their hands, on which they broke them easily. He then addressed them in these words: " My sons, if you are of one mind, and unite to assist each other, you will be as this faggot, uninjured by all the attempts of your enemies; but if you are divided among yourselves, you will be broken as easily as these sticks."

THE BAT AND THE WEASELS.

A BAT falling upon the ground was caught by a Weasel, of whom he earnestly besought his life. The Weasel refused, saying, that he was by nature the enemy of all birds. The Bat assured him that he was not a bird, but a mouse, and thus saved his life. Shortly afterwards the Bat again fell on the ground, and was caught by another Weasel, whom he likewise entreated not to eat him. The Weasel said that he had a special hostility to mice. The Bat assured him that he was not a mouse, but a bat; and thus a second time escaped.

It is wise to turn circumstances to good account.

THE COCK AND THE JEWEL.

A Cock, scratching for food for himself and his hens, found a precious stone; on which he said : "If your owner had found thee, and not I, he would have taken thee up, and have set thee in thy first estate ; but I have found thee for no purpose. I would rather have one barleycorn than all the jewels in the world."

THE SWALLOW AND THE CROW.

The Swallow and the Crow had a contention about their plumage. The Crow put an end to the dispute by saying : "Your feathers are all very well in the spring, but mine protect me against the winter."

Fine weather friends are not worth much.

THE KINGDOM OF THE LION.

THE beasts of the field and forest had a Lion as their king. He was neither wrathful, cruel, nor tyrannical, but just and gentle as a king could be. He made during his reign a royal proclamation for a general assembly of all the birds and beasts, and drew up conditions for an universal league, in which the Wolf and the Lamb, the Panther and the Kid, the Tiger and the Stag, the Dog and the Hare, should live together in perfect peace and amity. The Hare said, "Oh, how I have longed to see this day, in which the weak shall take their place with impunity by the side of the strong."

THE TRAVELLER AND HIS DOG.

A TRAVELLER, about to set out on his journey, saw his Dog stand at the door stretching himself. He asked him sharply : "What do you stand gaping there for ? Everything is ready but you; so come with me instantly." The Dog, wagging his tail, replied : " O, master ! I am quite ready ; it is you for whom I am waiting."

The loiterer often imputes delay to his more active friend.

THE ANTS AND THE GRASSHOPPER.

THE Ants were employing a fine winter's day in drying grain collected in the summer time. A Grasshopper, perishing with famine, passed by and earnestly begged for a little food. The Ants enquired of him, " Why did you not treasure up food during the summer ? " He replied, " I had not leisure enough. I passed the days in singing." They then said in derision : " If you were foolish enough to sing all the summer, you must dance supperless to bed in the winter."

THE HARE AND THE TORTOISE.

A HARE one day ridiculed the short feet and slow pace of the Tortoise. The latter, laughing, said : "Though you be swift as the wind, I will beat you in a race." The Hare, deeming her assertion to be simply impossible, assented to the proposal ; and they agreed that the Fox should choose the course, and fix the goal. On the day appointed for the race they started together. The Tortoise never for a moment stopped, but went on with a slow but steady pace straight to the end of the course. The Hare, trusting to his native swiftness, cared little about the race, and lying down by the wayside, fell fast asleep. At last waking up, and moving as fast as he could, he saw the Tortoise had reached the goal, and was comfortably dozing after her fatigue.

THE CHARCOAL-BURNER AND THE FULLER.

A CHARCOAL-BURNER carried on his trade in his own house. One day he met a friend, a Fuller, and entreated him to come and live with him, saying, that they should be far better neighbours, and that their housekeeping expenses would be lessened. The Fuller replied, "The arrangement is impossible as far as I am concerned, for whatever I should whiten, you would immediately blacken again with your charcoal."

Like will draw like.

THE BOY HUNTING LOCUSTS.

A BOY was hunting for locusts. He had caught a goodly number, when he saw a Scorpion, and, mistaking him for a locust, reached out his hand to take him. The Scorpion, showing his sting, said : "If you had but touched me, my friend, you would have lost me, and all your locusts too !"

THE FISHERMAN PIPING.

A FISHERMAN skilled in music took his flute and his nets to the sea-shore. Standing on a projecting rock he played several tunes, in the hope that the fish, attracted by his melody, would of their own accord dance into his net, which he had placed below. At last, having long waited in vain, he laid aside his flute, and casting his net into the sea, made an excellent haul of fish. When he saw them leaping about in the net upon the rock he said : "O you most perverse creatures, when I piped you would not dance, but now that I have ceased you do so merrily."

THE DOG AND THE SHADOW.

A Dog, crossing a bridge over a stream with a piece of flesh in his mouth, saw his own shadow in the water, and took it for that of another Dog, with a piece of meat double his own in size. He therefore let go his own, and fiercely attacked the other Dog, to get his larger piece from him. He thus lost both: that which he grasped at in the water, because it was a shadow; and his own, because the stream swept it away.

HERCULES AND THE WAGGONER.

A Carter was driving a waggon along a country lane, when the wheels sank down deep into a rut. The rustic driver, stupefied and aghast, stood looking at the waggon, and did nothing but utter loud cries to Hercules to come and help him. Hercules, it is said, appeared, and thus addressed him :—" Put your shoulders to the wheels, my man. Goad on your bullocks, and never more pray to me for help, until you have done your best to help yourself, or depend upon it you will henceforth pray in vain."

Self-help is the best help.

THE MOLE AND HIS MOTHER.

A Mole, a creature blind from its birth, once said to his mother : " I am sure that I can see, mother !" In the desire to prove to him his mistake, his mother placed before him a few grains of frankincense, and asked, " What is it ? " The young Mole said, " It is a pebble." His mother exclaimed : " My son, I am afraid that you are not only blind, but that you have lost your sense of smell."

THE HERDSMAN AND THE LOST BULL.

A Herdsman tending kine in a forest, lost a Bull calf from the fold. After a long and fruitless search, he made a vow that, if he could only discover the thief who had stolen the Calf, he would offer a lamb in sacrifice to Hermes, Pan, and the Guardian Deities of the forest. Not long afterwards, as he ascended a small hillock, he saw at its foot a Lion feeding on the Calf. Terrified at the sight, he lifted his eyes and his hands to heaven, and said : " Just now I vowed to offer a lamb to the Guardian Deities of the forest if I could only find out who had robbed me ; but now that I have discovered the thief, I would willingly add a full-grown Bull to the Calf I have lost, if I may only secure my own escape from him in safety."

THE FAWN AND HIS MOTHER.

A YOUNG Fawn once said to his mother, " You are larger than a dog, and swifter, and more used to running, and you have, too, your horns as a defence; why, then, O Mother! are you always in such a terrible fright of the hounds?" She smiled, and said: "I know full well, my son, that all you say is true. I have the advantages you mention, but yet when I hear only the bark of a single dog I feel ready to faint, and fly away as fast as I can."

No arguments will give courage to the coward.

THE ASS, THE FOX, AND THE LION.

THE Ass and the Fox having entered into partnership together for their mutual protection, went out into the forest to hunt.   They had not proceeded far, when they met a Lion.   The Fox, seeing the imminency of the danger, approached the Lion, and promised to contrive for him the capture of the Ass, if he would pledge his word that his own life should not be endangered.   On his assuring him that he would not injure him, the Fox led the Ass to a deep pit, and contrived that he should fall into it.   The Lion seeing that the Ass was secured, immediately clutched the Fox, and then attacked the Ass at his leisure.

_____

THE FLIES AND THE HONEY POT.

A JAR of Honey having been upset in a housekeeper's room, a number of flies were attracted by its sweetness, and placing their feet in it, ate it greedily.   Their feet, however, became so smeared with the honey that they could not use their wings, nor release themselve. id were suffocated.   Just as they were expiring, they exclaimed, " O foolish creatures that we are, for the sake of a little pleasure we have destroyed ourselves."

Pleasure bought with pains, hurts.

_____

THE LIONESS.

A CONTROVERSY prevailed among the beasts of the field, as to which of the animals deserved the most credit for producing the greatest number of whelps at a birth. They rushed clamorously into the presence of the Lioness, and demanded of her the settlement of the dispute. " And you," they said, " how many sons have you at a birth ? "   The Lioness laughed at them, and said : "Why ! I have only one ; but that one is altogether a thorough-bred Lion."

The value is in the worth, not in the number.

THE FARMER AND THE SNAKE.

A FARMER found in the winter time a Snake stiff and frozen with cold. He had compassion on it, and taking it up placed it in his bosom. The Snake on being thawed by the warmth quickly revived, when, resuming its natural instincts, he bit his benefactor, inflicting on him a mortal wound. The Farmer said with his latest breath, " I am rightly served for pitying a scoundrel ! "

The greatest benefits will not bind the ungrateful.

THE MAN AND THE LION.

A MAN and a lion travelled together through the forest. They soon began to boast of their respective superiority to each other in strength and prowess. As they were disputing, they passed a statue, carved in stone, which represented "a Lion strangled by a Man." The traveller pointed to it and said : "See there ! How strong we are, and how we prevail over even the king of beasts." The Lion replied : " That statue was made by one of you men. If we Lions knew how to erect statues, you would see the Man placed under the paw of the Lion."

One story is good, till another is told.

THE POMEGRANATE, APPLE TREE, AND BRAMBLE.

THE Pomegranate and Apple-tree disputed as to which was the most beautiful. When their strife was at its height, a Bramble from the neighbouring hedge lifted up its voice, and said in a boastful tone : " Pray, my dear friends, in my presence at least cease from such vain disputings."

THE FARMER AND THE STORK.

A FARMER placed nets on his newly-sown plough lands, and caught a quantity of Cranes, which came to pick up his seed. With them he trapped a Stork also. The Stork having his leg fractured by the net, earnestly besought the Farmer to spare his life. "Pray, save me, Master," he said, "and let me go free this once. My broken limb should excite your pity. Besides, I am no Crane, I am a Stork, a bird of excellent character; and see how I love and slave for my father and mother. Look too, at my feathers, they are not the least like to those of a Crane." The Farmer laughed aloud, and said, "It may be all as you say; I only know this, I have taken you with these robbers, the Cranes, and you must die in their company."

Birds of a feather flock together.

THE MOUNTAIN IN LABOUR.

A MOUNTAIN was once greatly agitated. Loud groans and noises were heard; and crowds of people came from all parts to see what was the matter. While they were assembled in anxious expectation of some terrible calamity, out came a Mouse.

Don't make much ado about nothing.

THE BEAR AND THE FOX.

A BEAR boasted very much of his philanthropy, saying "that of all animals he was the most tender in his regard for man, for he had such respect for him, that he would not even ·touch his dead body." A Fox hearing these words said with a smile to the Bear, "Oh! that you would eat the dead and not the living."

THE TORTOISE AND THE EAGLE.

A TORTOISE, lazily basking in the sun, complained to the sea-birds of her hard fate, that no one would teach her to fly. An Eagle hovering near, heard her lamentation, and demanded what reward she would give him, if he would take her aloft, and float her in the air. "I will give you," she said, "all the riches of the Red Sea." "I will teach you to fly then," said the Eagle; and taking her up in his talons, he carried her almost to the clouds, —when suddenly letting her go, she fell on a lofty mountain, and dashed her shell to pieces. The Tortoise exclaimed in the moment of death: "I have deserved my present fate; for what had I to do with wings and clouds, who can with difficulty move about on the earth?"

If men had all they wished, they would be often ruined.

THE FOX AND THE GOAT.

A Fox having fallen into a deep well, was detained a prisoner there, as he could find no means of escape. A Goat, overcome with thirst, came to the same well, and, seeing the Fox, enquired if the water was good. The Fox, concealing his sad plight under a merry guise, indulged in a lavish praise of the water, saying it was beyond measure excellent, and encouraged him to descend. The Goat, mindful only of his thirst, thoughtlessly jumped down, when just as he quenched his thirst, the Fox informed him of the difficulty they were both in, and suggested a scheme for their common escape. "If," said he, "you will place your fore-feet upon the wall, and bend your head, I will run up your back and escape, and will help you out afterwards." On the Goat readily assenting to this second proposal, the Fox leapt upon his back, and steadying himself with the Goat's horns, reached in safety the mouth of the well, when he immediately made off as fast as he could. The Goat upbraided him with the breach of his bargain, when he turned round and cried out : " You foolish old fellow ! If you had as many brains in your head as you have hairs in your beard, you would never have gone down before you had inspected the way up, nor have exposed yourself to dangers from which you had no means of escape."

Look before you leap.

THE RAVEN AND THE SWAN.

A Raven saw a Swan, and desired to secure for himself a like beauty of plumage. Supposing that his splendid white colour arose from his washing in the water in which he swam, the Raven left the altars in the neighbourhood of which he picked up his living, and took up his abode in the lakes and pools. But cleansing his feathers as often as he would, he could not change their colour, while through want of food he perished.

Change of habit cannot alter Nature.

THE THIRSTY PIGEON.

A Pigeon, oppressed by excessive thirst, saw a goblet of water painted on a sign-board. Not supposing it to be only a picture, she flew towards it with a loud whirr, and unwittingly dashed against the sign-board and jarred herself terribly. Having broken her wings by the blow, she fell to the ground, and was caught by one of the bystanders.

Zeal should not outrun discretion.

THE DOG IN THE MANGER.

A Dog lay in a manger, and by his growling and snapping prevented the oxen from eating the hay which had been placed for them. "What a selfish Dog!" said one of them to his companions; "he cannot eat the hay himself, and yet refuses to allow those to eat who can."

THE OXEN AND THE AXLE-TREES.

A heavy waggon was being dragged along a country lane by a team of oxen. The axle-trees groaned and creaked terribly: when the oxen turning round, thus addressed the wheels. "Hullo there! why do you make so much noise? We bear all the labour, and we, not you, ought to cry out."

Those who suffer most cry out the least.

THE FARMER AND THE CRANES.

Some Cranes made their feeding grounds on some plough lands newly sown with wheat. For a long time the Farmer, brandishing an empty sling, chased them away by the terror he inspired; but when the birds found that the sling was only swung in the air, they ceased to take any notice of it, and would not move. The Farmer on seeing this, charged his sling with stones, and killed a great number. They at once forsook his plough-lands, and cried to each other, "It is time for us to be off to Liliput : for this man is no longer content to scare us, but begins to show us in earnest what he can do."

If words suffice not, blows must follow.

THE SICK LION.

A Lion being unable from old age and infirmities to provide himself with food by force, resolved to do so by artifice. He betook himself to his den, and lying down there, pretended to be sick, taking care that his sickness should be publicly known. The beasts expressed their sorrow, and came one by one to his den to visit him, when the Lion devoured them. After many of the beasts had thus disappeared, the Fox discovered the trick, and presenting himself to the Lion, stood on the outside of the cave, at a respectful distance, and asked of him how he did; to whom he replied, "I am very middling, but why do you stand without? pray enter within to talk with me." The Fox replied, "No, thank you, I notice that there are many prints of feet entering your cave, but I see no trace of any returning."

He is wise who is warned by the misfortunes of others.

THE BEAR AND THE TWO TRAVELLERS.

Two men were travelling together, when a Bear suddenly met them on their path.   One of them climbed up quickly into a tree, and concealed himself in the branches. The other, seeing that he must be attacked, fell flat on the ground, and when the Bear came up and felt him with his snout, and smelt him all over, he held his breath, and feigned the appearance of death as much as he could.   The Bear soon left him, for it is said he will not touch a dead body.   When he was quite gone the other traveller descended from the tree, and accosting his friend, jocularly inquired " what it was the Bear had whispered in his ear ? "   He replied,   " He gave me this advice : Never travel with a friend who deserts you at the approach of danger."

Misfortune tests the sincerity of friends.

THE FOX WHO HAD LOST HIS TAIL.

A Fox caught in a trap, escaped with the loss of his " brush."   Henceforth feeling his life a burden from the shame and ridicule to which he was exposed, he schemed to bring all the other Foxes into a like condition with himself, that in the common loss he might the better conceal his own deprivation.   He assembled a good many Foxes, and publicly advised them to cut off their tails, saying " that they would not only look much better without them, but that they would get rid of the weight of the brush, which was a very great inconvenience."   One of them interrupting him said, " If you had not yourself lost your tail, my friend, you would not thus counsel us."

THE CAT AND THE COCK.

A CAT caught a Cock, and took counsel with himself how he might find a reasonable excuse for eating him. He accused him as being a nuisance to men, by crowing in the night time, and not permitting them to sleep. The Cock defended himself by saying, that he did this for the benefit of men, that they might rise betimes for their labours. The Cat replied, "Although you abound in specious apologies, I shall not remain supperless;" and he made a meal of him.

THE WOLF IN SHEEP'S CLOTHING.

ONCE upon a time a Wolf resolved to disguise his nature by his habit, that so he might get food without stint. Encased in the skin of a sheep, he pastured with the flock, beguiling the shepherd by his artifice. In the evening he was shut up by the shepherd in the fold ; the gate was closed, and the entrance made thoroughly secure. The shepherd coming into the fold during the night to provide food for the morrow, caught up the Wolf, instead of a sheep, and killed him with his knife in the fold.

Harm seek, harm find.

THE GOAT AND THE GOATHERD.

A GOATHERD had sought to bring back a stray goat to his flock. He whistled and sounded his horn in vain ; the straggler paid no attention to the summons. At last the Goatherd threw a stone, and breaking its horn besought the Goat not to tell his master. The Goat replied, "Why, you silly fellow, the horn will speak though I be silent."

Do not attempt to hide things which cannot be hidden.

THE BOASTING TRAVELLER.

A MAN who had travelled in foreign lands, boasted very much, on returning to his own country, of the many wonderful and heroic things he had done in the different places he had visited. Among other things, he said that when he was at Rhodes he had leaped to such a distance that no man of his day could leap anywhere near him—and as to that, there were in Rhodes many persons who saw him do it, and whom he could call as witnesses. One of the bystanders interrupting him, said, "Now, my good man, if this be all true there is no need of witnesses. Suppose this to be Rhodes; and now for your leap."

THE LION IN LOVE.

A LION demanded the daughter of a woodcutter in marriage. The Father, unwilling to grant, and yet afraid to refuse his request, hit upon this expedient to rid himself of his importunities. He expressed his willingness to accept him as the suitor of his daughter on one condition; that he should allow him to extract his teeth, and cut off his claws, as his daughter was fearfully afraid of both. The Lion cheerfully assented to the proposal: when however he next repeated his request, the woodman, no longer afraid, set upon him with his club, and drove him away into the forest.

THE MISER.

A MISER sold all that he had, and bought a lump of gold, which he took and buried in a hole dug in the ground by the side of an old wall, and went daily to look at it. One of his workmen, observing his frequent visits to the spot, watched his movements, discovered the secret of the hidden treasure, and digging down, came to the lump of gold, and stole it. The Miser, on his next visit, found the hole empty, and began to tear his hair, and to make loud lamentations. A neighbour, seeing him overcome with grief, and learning the cause, said, "Pray do not grieve so; but go and take a stone, and place it in the hole, and fancy that the gold is still lying there. It will do you quite the same service; for when the gold was there, you had it not, as you did not make the slightest use of it."

THE PORKER, THE SHEEP, AND THE GOAT.

A YOUNG Pig was shut up in a fold-yard with a Goat and a Sheep. On one occasion the shepherd laid hold of him, when he grunted, and squeaked, and resisted violently. The Sheep and the Goat complained of his distressing cries, and said, " He often handles us, and we do not cry out." To this he replied, " Your handling and mine are very different things. He catches you only for your wool, or your milk, but he lays hold on me for my very life."

THE BOY AND THE FILBERTS.

A Boy put his hand into a pitcher full of filberts. He grasped as many as he could possibly hold, but when he endeavoured to pull out his hand, he was prevented from doing so by the neck of the pitcher. Unwilling to lose his filberts, and yet unable to withdraw his hand, he burst into tears, and bitterly lamented his disappointment. A bystander said to him, " Be satisfied with half the quantity, and you will readily draw out your hand."

Do not attempt too much at once.

THE FROGS ASKING FOR A KING.

THE Frogs, grieved at having no established Ruler, sent ambassadors to Jupiter entreating for a King. He, perceiving their simplicity, cast down a huge log into the lake. The Frogs, terrified at the splash occasioned by its fall, hid themselves in the depths of the pool. But no sooner did they see that the huge log continued motionless, than they swam again to the top of the water, dismissed their fears, and came so to despise it as to climb up, and to squat upon it. After some time they began to think themselves ill-treated in the appointment of so inert a Ruler, and sent a second deputation to Jupiter to pray that he would set over them another sovereign. He then gave them an Eel to govern them. When the Frogs discovered his easy good-nature, they yet a third time sent to Jupiter to beg that he would once more choose for them another King. Jupiter, displeased at their complaints, sent a Heron, who preyed upon the Frogs day by day till there were none left to croak upon the lake.

THE LABOURER AND THE SNAKE.

A SNAKE, having made his hole close to the porch of a cottage, inflicted a severe bite on the Cottager's infant son, of which he died, to the great grief of his parents. The father resolved to kill the Snake, and the next day, on its coming out of its hole for food, took up his axe; but, making too much haste to hit him as he wriggled away, missed his head, and cut off only the end of his tail. After some time the Cottager, afraid lest the Snake should bite him also, endeavoured to make peace, and placed some bread and salt in his hole. The Snake, slightly hissing, said: "There can henceforth be no peace between us; for whenever I see you I shall remember the loss of my tail, and whenever you see me you will be thinking of the death of your son."

No one truly forgets injuries in the presence of him who caused the injury.

THE LION, THE MOUSE, AND THE FOX.

A LION, fatigued by the heat of a summer's day, fell fast asleep in his den. A Mouse ran over his mane and ears, and woke him from his slumbers. He rose up and shook himself in great wrath, and searched every corner of his den to find the Mouse. A Fox seeing him, said: "A fine Lion you are, to be frightened of a Mouse." "'Tis not the Mouse I fear," said the Lion; "I resent his familiarity and ill-breeding."

Little liberties are great offences.

THE HORSE AND GROOM.

A Groom used to spend whole days in currycombing and rubbing down his Horse, but at the same time stole his oats, and sold them for his own profit. "Alas!" said the Horse, "if you really wish me to be in good condition, you should groom me less, and feed me more."

Honesty is the best policy.

THE ASS AND THE MULE.

A Muleteer set forth on a journey, driving before him an Ass and a Mule, both well laden. The Ass, as long as he travelled along the plain, carried his load with ease; but when he begun to ascend the steep path of the mountain, he felt his load to be more than he could bear. He entreated his companion to relieve him of a small portion, that he might carry home the rest; but the Mule paid no attention to the request. The Ass shortly afterwards fell down dead under his burden. The Muleteer, not knowing what else to do in so wild a region, placed upon the Mule the load carried by the Ass in addition to his own, and at the top of all placed the hide of the Ass, after he had flayed him. The Mule, groaning beneath his heavy burden, said thus to himself, " I am treated according to my deserts. If I had only been willing to assist the Ass a little in his need, I should not now be bearing, together with his burden, himself as well."

THE ASS AND THE LAP-DOG.

A MAN had an Ass, and a Maltese Lap-dog, a very great beauty. The Ass was left in a stable, and had plenty of oats and hay to eat, just as any other Ass would. The Lap-dog knew many tricks, and was a great favourite with his master, who often fondled him ; and seldom went out to dine or to sup without bringing him home some tid-bit to eat, when he frisked and jumped about him in a manner pleasant to see. The Ass, on the contrary, had much work to do, in grinding the corn-mill, and in carrying wood from the forest or burdens from the farm. He often lamented his own hard fate, and contrasted it with the luxury and idleness of the Lap-dog, till at last one day he broke his cords and halter, and galloped into his master's house, kicking up his heels without measure, and frisking and fawning as well as he could. He next tried to jump about his master as he had seen the Lap-dog do, but he broke the table, and smashed all the dishes upon it to atoms. He then attempted to lick his master, and jumped upon his back. The servants hearing the strange hubbub, and perceiving the danger of their master, quickly relieved him, and drove out the Ass to his stable, with kicks, and clubs, and cuffs. The Ass, as he returned to his stall beaten nearly to death, thus lamented: "I have brought it all on myself! Why could I not have been contented to labour with my companions, and not wish to be idle all the day like that useless little Lap-dog!"

THE OXEN AND THE BUTCHERS.

THE Oxen once on a time sought to destroy the Butchers, who practised a trade destructive to their race. They assembled on a certain day to carry out their purpose, and sharpened their horns for the contest. One of them, an exceedingly old one (for many a field had he ploughed), thus spoke: "These Butchers, it is true, slaughter us, but they do so with skilful hands, and with no unnecessary pain. If we get rid of them, we shall fall into the hands of unskilful operators, and thus suffer a double death: for you may be assured, that though all the Butchers should perish, yet will men never want beef."

Do not be in a hurry to change one evil for another.

THE SHEPHERD'S BOY AND WOLF.

A SHEPHERD-BOY, who watched a flock of sheep near a village, brought out the villagers three or four times by crying out, "Wolf! Wolf!" and when his neighbours came to help him, laughed at them for their pains. The Wolf, however, did truly come at last. The Shepherd-boy, now really alarmed, shouted in an agony of terror:

"Pray, do come and help me; the wolf is killing the sheep;" but no one paid any heed to his cries, nor rendered any assistance. The Wolf, having no cause of fear, took it easily, and lacerated or destroyed the whole flock.

There is no believing a liar, even when he speaks the truth.

THE BOYS AND THE FROGS.

SOME Boys, playing near a pond, saw a number of Frogs in the water, and beagn to pelt them with stones. They killed several of them, when one of the Frogs, lifting his head out of the water, cried out: "Pray stop, my boys: what is sport to you, is death to us."

THE SALT MERCHANT AND HIS ASS.

A PEDLAR, dealing in salt, drove his Ass to the sea-shore to buy salt. His road home lay across a stream, in passing which his Ass, making a false step, fell by accident into the water, and rose up again with his load considerably lighter, as the water melted the salt. The Pedlar retraced his steps, and refilled his panniers with a larger quantity of salt than before. When he came again to the stream, the Ass fell down on purpose in the same spot, and, regaining his feet with the weight of his load much diminished, brayed triumphantly as if he had obtained what he desired. The Pedlar saw through his trick, and drove him for the third time to the coast, where he bought a cargo of sponges instead of salt. The Ass, again playing the knave, when he reached the stream, fell down on purpose, when the sponges becoming swollen with the water, his load was very greatly increased; and thus his trick recoiled on himself in fitting to his back a doubled burden.

THE MISCHIEVOUS DOG.

A DOG used to run up quietly to the heels of everyone he met, and to bite them without notice. His master suspended a bell about his neck, that he might give notice of his presence wherever he went. The Dog grew proud of his bell, and went tinkling it all over the market-place. An old hound said to him: "Why do you make such an exhibition of yourself? That bell that you carry is not, believe me, any order of merit, but, on the contrary, a mark of disgrace, a public notice to all men to avoid you as an ill-mannered dog."

Notoriety is often mistaken for fame.

THE GOATHERD AND THE WILD GOATS.

A GOATHERD, driving his flock from their pasture at eventide, found some wild goats mingled among them, and shut them up together with his own for the night. On the morrow it snowed very hard, so that he could not take the herd to their usual feeding-places, but was obliged to keep them in the fold. He gave his own goats just sufficient food to keep them alive, but fed the strangers more abundantly, in the hope of enticing them to stay with him, and of making them his own. When the thaw set in, he led them all out to feed, and the wild goats scampered away as fast as they could to the mountains. The Goatherd taxed them with their ingratitude in leaving him, when during the storm he had taken more care of them than of his own herd. One of them turning about said to him, "That is the very reason why we are so cautious; for if you yesterday treated us better than the Goats you have had so long, it is plain also that if others came after us, you would, in the same manner, prefer them to ourselves."

Old friends cannot with impunity be sacrificed for new ones.

THE MAN AND HIS TWO SWEETHEARTS.

A MIDDLE-AGED man, whose hair had begun to turn grey, courted two women at the same time. One of them was young; and the other well advanced in years. The elder woman, ashamed to be courted by a man younger than herself, made a point, whenever her admirer visited her, to pull out some portion of his black hairs. The younger, on the contrary, not wishing to become the wife of an old man, was equally zealous in removing every grey hair she could find. Thus it came to pass, that between them both he very soon found that he had not a hair left on his head.

Those who seek to please everybody please nobody.

THE SICK STAG.

A sick Stag lay down in a quiet corner of its pasture-ground. His companions came in great numbers to inquire after his health, and each one helped himself to a share of the food which had been placed for his use ; so that he died, not from his sickness, but from the failure of the means of living.

Evil companions bring more hurt than profit.

THE BOY AND THE NETTLES.

A Boy was stung by a Nettle. He ran home and told his mother, saying, "Although it pains me so much, I did but touch it ever so gently." "That was just it," said his mother, "which caused it to sting you. The next time you touch a Nettle, grasp it boldly, and it will be as soft as silk to your hand, and not in the least hurt you."

Whatever you do, do with all your might.

THE ASTRONOMER.

An Astronomer used to go out of a night to observe the stars. One evening, as he wandered through the suburbs with his whole attention fixed on the sky, he fell unawares into a deep well. While he lamented and bewailed his sores and bruises, and cried loudly for help, a neighbour ran to the well, and learning what had happened, said: "Hark ye, old fellow, why, in striving to pry into what is in heaven, do you not manage to see what is on earth?"

THE WOLVES AND THE SHEEP.

"Why should there always be this internecine and implacable warfare between us?" said the Wolves to the Sheep. "Those evil-disposed Dogs have much to answer for. They always bark whenever we approach you, and attack us before we have done any harm. If you would only dismiss them from your heels, there might soon be treaties of peace and of reconciliation between us." The Sheep, poor silly creatures! were easily beguiled, and dismissed the Dogs. The Wolves destroyed the unguarded flock at their own pleasure.

THE CAT AND THE BIRDS.

A Cat, hearing that the Birds in a certain aviary were ailing, dressed himself up as a physician, and, taking with him his cane and the instruments becoming his profession, went to the aviary, knocked at the door, and inquired of the inmates how they all did, saying that if they were ill, he would be happy to prescribe for them and cure them. They replied, "We are all very well, and shall continue so, if you will only be good enough to go away, and leave us as we are."

THE VAIN JACKDAW.

JUPITER determined, it is said, to create a sovereign over the birds; and made proclamation that, on a certain day, they should all present themselves before him, when he would himself choose the most beautiful among them to be king. The Jackdaw, knowing his own ugliness, searched through the woods and fields, and collected the feathers which had fallen from the wings of his companions, and stuck them in all parts of his body, hoping thereby to make himself the most beautiful of all. When the appointed day arrived, and the birds had assembled before Jupiter, the Jackdaw also made his appearance in his many-feathered finery. On Jupiter proposing to make him king, on account of the beauty of his plumage, the birds indignantly protested, and each plucking from him his own feathers, the Jackdaw was again nothing but a Jackdaw.

THE KID AND THE WOLF.

A KID standing on the roof of a house, out of harm's way, saw a Wolf passing by : and immediately began to taunt and revile him. The Wolf, looking up, said : "Sirrah ! I hear thee : yet it is not thou who mockest me, but the roof on which thou art standing."

Time and place often give the advantage to the weak over the strong.

THE OLD WOMAN AND THE PHYSICIAN.

AN old woman having lost the use of her eyes, called in a Physician to heal them, and made this bargain with him in the presence of witnesses : that if he should cure her blindness, he should receive from her a sum of money ; but if her infirmity remained, she should give him nothing. This agreement being entered into, the Physician, time after time, applied his salve to her eyes, and on every visit taking something away, stole by little and little all her property : and when he had got all she had, he healed her, and demanded the promised payment. The old woman, when she recovered her sight and saw none of her goods in her house, would give him nothing. The Physician insisted on his claim, and, as she still refused, summoned her before the Archons. The old woman standing up in the Court thus spoke :—"This man here speaks the truth in what he says ; for I did promise to give him a sum of money, if I should recover my sight : but if I continued blind, I was to give him nothing. Now he declares 'that I am healed.' I on the contrary affirm 'that I am still blind ;' for when I lost the use of my eyes, I saw in my house various chattels and valuable goods : but now, though he swears I am cured of my blindness, I am not able to see a single thing in it."

THE OX AND THE FROG.

An Ox drinking at a pool, trod on a brood of young
frogs, and crushed one of them to death. The mother
coming up, and missing one of her sons, inquired of his
brothers what had become of him. "He is dead, dear
mother; for just now a very huge beast with four great
feet came to the pool, and crushed him to death with his
cloven heel." The Frog, puffing herself out, inquired,
"if the beast was as big as that in size." "Cease,
mother, to puff yourself out," said her son, "and do not
be angry; for you would, I assure you, sooner burst than
successfully imitate the hugeness of that monster."

THE FARMER AND HIS SONS.

A FARMER being on the point of death, wished to insure from his sons the same attention to his farm as he had himself given it. He called them to his bedside, and said, " My sons, there is a great treasure hidden in one of my vineyards." The sons after his death took their spades and mattocks, and carefully dug over every portion of their land. They found no treasure, but the vines repaid their labour by an extraordinary and super- abundant crop.

THE HEIFER AND THE OX.

A HEIFER saw an Ox hard at work harnessed to a plough, and tormented him with reflections on his unhappy fate in being compelled to labour. Shortly afterwards, at the harvest home, the owner released the Ox from his yoke, but bound the Heifer with cords, and led her away to the altar to be slain in honour of the festival. The Ox saw what was being done, and said with a smile to the Heifer: "For this you were allowed to live in idleness, because you were presently to be sacrificed."

THE FIGHTING COCKS AND THE EAGLE.

Two Game Cocks were fiercely fighting for the mastery of the farm-yard. One at last put the other to flight. The vanquished Cock skulked away and hid himself in a quiet corner. The conqueror, flying up to a high wall, flapped his wings and crowed exultingly with all his might. An Eagle sailing through the air pounced upon him, and carried him off in his talons. The vanquished Cock immediately came out of his corner, and ruled henceforth with undisputed mastery.

Pride goes before destruction.

THE CHARGER AND THE MILLER.

A CHARGER, feeling the infirmities of age, betook him to a mill instead of going out to battle. But when he was compelled to grind instead of serving in the wars, he bewailed his change of fortune, and called to mind his former state, saying, " Ah ! Miller, I had indeed to go campaigning before, but I was barbed from counter to tail, and a man went along to groom me; and now, I cannot tell what ailed me to prefer the mill before the battle." " Forbear," said the Miller to him, " harping on what you were of yore, for it is the common lot of mortals to sustain the ups and downs of fortune."

THE FOX AND THE MONKEY.

A MONKEY once danced in an assembly of the Beasts, and so pleased them all by his performance that they elected him their King. A Fox envying him the honour, discovered a piece of meat lying in a trap, and leading the Monkey to the place where it was, said " that she had found a store, but had not used it, but had kept it for him as a treasure trove of his kingdom, and counselled him to lay hold of it." The Monkey approached carelessly, and was caught in the trap ; and on his accusing the Fox of purposely leading him into the snare, she replied, " O Monkey, and are you, with such a mind as yours, going to be King over the Beasts ? "

THE HORSE AND HIS RIDER.

A HORSE Soldier took the utmost pains with his charger. As long as the war lasted, he looked upon him as his fellow-helper in all emergencies, and fed him carefully with hay and corn. When the war was over, he only allowed him chaff to eat, and made him carry heavy loads of wood, and subjected him to much slavish drudgery and ill-treatment. War, however, being again proclaimed, and the trumpet summoning him to his standard, the soldier put on his charger its military trappings, and mounted, being clad in his heavy coat of mail. The Horse fell down straightway under the weight, no longer equal to the burden, and said to his master, " You must now e'en go to the war on foot, for you have transformed me from a Horse into an Ass ; and how can you expect that I can again turn in a moment from an Ass to a Horse?"

THE BELLY AND THE MEMBERS.

THE members of the Body rebelled against the Belly, and said, "Why should we be perpetually engaged in administering to your wants, while you do nothing but take your rest, and enjoy yourself in luxury and self-indulgence?" The members carried out their resolve, and refused their assistance to the Body. The whole Body quickly became debilitated, and the hands, feet, mouth, and eyes, when too late, repented of their folly.

THE WIDOW AND HER LITTLE MAIDENS.

A WIDOW woman, fond of cleaning, had two little maidens to wait on her. She was in the habit of waking them early in the morning, at cockcrow. The maidens being aggrieved by such excessive labour, resolved to kill the cock who roused their mistress so early. When they had done this, they found that they had only prepared for themselves greater troubles, for their mistress, no longer hearing the hour from the cock, woke them up to their work in the middle of the night.

THE VINE AND THE GOAT.

A VINE was luxuriant in the time of vintage with leaves
and grapes. A Goat, passing by, nibbled its young tendrils and its leaves. The Vine addressed him, and said :
" Why do you thus injure me without a cause, and crop
my leaves ? Is there no young grass left ? But I shall
not have to wait long for my just revenge ; for if you now
should crop my leaves, and cut me down to my root, I
shall provide the wine to pour over you when you are led
as a victim to the sacrifice."

JUPITER AND THE MONKEY.

JUPITER issued a proclamation to all the beasts of the
forest, and promised a royal reward to the one whose
offspring should be deemed the handsomest. The Mon-

key came with the rest, and presented, with all a mother's tenderness, a flat-nosed, hairless, ill-featured young Monkey as a candidate for the promised reward. A general laugh saluted her on the presentation of her son. She resolutely said, "I know not whether Jupiter will allot the prize to my son; but this I do know, that he is, at least in the eyes of me, his mother, the dearest, handsomest, and most beautiful of all."

THE HAWK, THE KITE, AND THE PIGEONS.

THE Pigeons, terrified by the appearance of a Kite, called upon the Hawk to defend them. He at once consented. When they had admitted him into the cote, they found that he made more havoc, and slew a larger number of them in one day, than the Kite could pounce upon in a whole year.

Avoid a remedy that is worse than the disease.

THE DOLPHINS, THE WHALES, AND THE SPRAT.

THE Dolphins and Whales waged a fierce warfare with each other. When the battle was at its height, a Sprat lifted its head out of the waves, and said that he would reconcile their differences, if they would accept him as an umpire. One of the Dolphins replied, "We would far rather be destroyed in our battle with each other, than admit any interference from you in our affairs."

THE SWALLOW, THE SERPENT, AND THE COURT OF JUSTICE.

A SWALLOW, returning from abroad, and ever fond of dwelling with men, built herself a nest in the wall of a Court of Justice, and there hatched seven young birds.

A Serpent gliding past the nest, from its hole in the wall, ate up the young unfledged nestlings. The Swallow, finding her nest empty, lamented greatly, and exclaimed : "Woe to me a stranger ! that in this place where all others' rights are protected, I alone should suffer wrong."

THE TWO POTS.

A RIVER carried down in its stream two Pots, one made of earthenware, and the other of brass. The Earthen Pot said to the Brass Pot, " Pray keep at a distance, and do not come near me ; for if you touch me ever so slightly, I shall be broken in pieces ; and besides, I by no means wish to come near you."

Equals make the best friends.

THE SHEPHERD AND THE WOLF.

A SHEPHERD once found the whelp of a Wolf, and brought it up, and after awhile taught it to steal lambs from the neighbouring flocks. The Wolf having shown himself an apt pupil, said to the Shepherd, " Since you have taught me to steal, you must keep a sharp look-out, or you will lose some of your own flock."

THE CRAB AND ITS MOTHER.

A CRAB said to her son, " Why do you walk so onesided, my child? It is far more becoming to go straightforward." The young Crab replied : " Quite true, dear mother ; and if you will show me the straight way, I will promise to walk in it." The mother tried in vain, and submitted without remonstrance to the reproof of her child.

Example is more powerful than precept.

THE FATHER AND HIS TWO DAUGHTERS.

A MAN had two daughters, the one married to a gardener, and the other to a tile-maker. After a time he went to the daughter who had married the gardener, and inquired how she was, and how all things went with her. She said, " All things are prospering with me, and I have only one wish, that there may be a heavy fall of rain, in order that the plants may be well watered." Not long after he went to the daughter who had married the tile-maker, and likewise inquired of her how she fared ; she replied, " I want for nothing, and have only one wish, that the dry weather may continue, and the sun shine hot and bright, so that the bricks might be dried." He said to her, " If your sister wishes for rain, and you for dry weather, with which of the two am I to join my wishes ? "

THE THIEF AND HIS MOTHER.

A BOY stole a lesson-book from one of his school-fellows, and took it home to his mother. She not only abstained from beating him, but encouraged him. He next time stole a cloak and brought it to her, when she yet further commended him. The Youth, advanced to man's estate, proceeded to steal things of greater value. At last he was taken in the very act, and having his hands bound behind him, was led away to the place of public execution. His mother followed in the crowd and violently beat her breast in sorrow, whereon the young man said, " I wish to say something to my mother in her ear." She came close to him, when he quickly seized her ear with his teeth and bit it off. The mother upbraided him as an unnatural child, whereon he replied, " Ah ! if you had beaten me, when I first stole and brought to you that lesson-book, I should not have come to this, nor have been thus led to a disgraceful death."

THE OLD MAN AND DEATH.

AN old man was employed in cutting wood in the forest, and, in carrying the faggots into the city for sale one day, being very wearied with his long journey, he sat down by the wayside, and, throwing down his load, besought " Death " to come. " Death " immediately appeared, in answer to his summons, and asked for what reason he had called him. The old man replied, " That, lifting up the load, you may place it again upon my shoulders."

THE FIR TREE AND THE BRAMBLE.

A FIR TREE said boastingly to the Bramble, " You are useful for nothing at all ; while I am everywhere used for roofs and houses." The Bramble made answer : " You, poor creature, if you would only call to mind the axes and saws which are about to hew you down, you would have reason to wish that you had grown up a Bramble, not a Fir Tree."

Better poverty without care, than riches with.

THE ÆTHIOP.

THE purchaser of a black servant was persuaded that the colour of his skin arose from dirt contracted through the neglect of his former masters. On bringing him home he resorted to every means of cleaning, and subjected him to incessant scrubbings. He caught a severe cold, but he never changed his colour nor complexion.

What's bred in the bone will stick to the flesh.

THE MOUSE, THE FROG, AND THE HAWK.

A MOUSE who always lived on the land, by an unlucky chance formed an intimate acquaintance with a Frog, who lived for the most part in the water. The Frog, one day intent on mischief, bound the foot of the Mouse tightly to his own. Thus joined together, the Frog first of all led his friend the Mouse to the meadow where they were accustomed to find their food. After this, he gradually led him towards the pool in which he lived, until he reached the very brink, when suddenly jumping in he dragged the Mouse with him. The Frog enjoyed the water amazingly, and swam croaking about, as if he had done a meritorious action. The unhappy Mouse was soon suffocated with the water, and his dead body floated about on the surface, tied to the foot of the Frog. A Hawk observed it, and, pouncing upon it with his talons, carried it up aloft. The Frog being still fastened to the leg of the Mouse, was also carried off a prisoner, and was eaten by the Hawk.

Harm hatch, harm catch.

THE FISHERMAN AND HIS NETS.

A FISHERMAN, engaged in his calling, made a very successful cast, and captured a great haul of fish. He managed by a skilful handling of his net to retain all the large fish, and to draw them to the shore ; but he could not prevent the smaller fish from falling back through the meshes of the net into the sea.

THE WOLF AND THE SHEEP.

A WOLF, sorely wounded and bitten by dogs, lay sick and maimed in his lair. Being in want of food, he called to a Sheep, who was passing, and asked him to fetch some water from a stream flowing close beside him. "For," he said, "if you will bring me drink, I will find means to provide myself with meat." "Yes," said the Sheep, "if I should bring you the draught, you would doubtless make me provide the meat also."

Hypocritical speeches are easily seen through.

THE OLD WOMAN AND THE WINE-JAR

AN Old Woman found an empty jar which had lately been full of prime old wine, and which still retained the fragrant smell of its former contents. She greedily placed it several times to her nose, and drawing it backwards and forwards said, "O most delicious ! How nice must the wine itself have been, when it leaves behind in the very vessel which contained it so sweet a perfume !"

The memory of a good deed lives.

THE MAN BITTEN BY A DOG.

A MAN who had been bitten by a Dog, went about in quest of some one who might heal him. A friend meeting him, and learning what he wanted, said, "If you would be cured, take a piece of bread, and dip it in the blood from your wound, and go and give it to the Dog that bit you." The man who had been bitten laughed at this advice, and said, "Why? If I should do so, it would be as if I should pray every Dog in the town to bite me."

Benefits bestowed upon the evil-disposed, increase their means of injuring you.

THE HUNTSMAN AND THE FISHERMAN.

A HUNTSMAN, returning with his dogs from the field, fell in by chance with a Fisherman, bringing home a basket well laden with fish. The Huntsman wished to have the fish ; and their owner experienced an equal longing for the contents of the game-bag. They quickly agreed to exchange the produce of their day's sport. Each was so well pleased with his bargain, that they made for some time the same exchange day after day. A neighbour said to them, "If you go on in this way, you will soon destroy, by frequent use, the pleasure of your exchange, and each will again wish to retain the fruits of his own sport."

Abstain and enjoy.

THE FOX AND THE CROW.

A CROW having stolen a bit of flesh, perched in a tree, and held it in her beak. A Fox seeing her, longed to possess himself of the flesh : and by a wily stratagem succeeded. " How handsome is the Crow," he exclaimed, " in the beauty of her shape and in the fairness of her complexion! Oh, if her voice were only equal to her beauty, she would deservedly be considered the Queen of Birds!" This he said deceitfully; but the Crow, anxious to refute the reflection cast upon her voice, set up a loud caw, and dropped the flesh. The Fox quickly picked it up, and thus addressed the Crow: " My good Crow, your voice is right enough, but your wit is wanting."

THE WIDOW AND THE SHEEP.

A CERTAIN poor Widow had one solitary Sheep. At shearing time, wishing to take his fleece, and to avoid expense, she sheared him herself, but used the shears so unskilfully, that with the fleece she sheared the flesh. The Sheep, writhing with pain, said, " Why do you hurt me so, Mistress? What weight can my blood add to the wool? If you want my flesh, there is the butcher, who will kill me in a trice; but if you want my fleece and wool, there is the shearer, who will shear and not hurt me."

The least outlay is not always the greatest gain.

THE PLAYFUL ASS.

AN Ass climbed up to the roof of a building, and, frisking about there, broke in the tiling. The owner went up after him, and quickly drove him down, beating him severely with a thick wooden cudgel. The Ass said, " Why, I saw the Monkey do this very thing yesterday, and you all laughed heartily, as if it afforded you very great amusement."

Those who do not know their right place must be taught it.

THE STAG IN THE OX-STALL.

A STAG, hardly pressed by the hounds, and blind through fear to the danger he was running into, took shelter in a farm-yard, and hid himself in a shed among the oxen. An Ox gave him this kindly warning : "O unhappy creature! why should you thus, of your own accord, incur destruction, and trust yourself in the house of your enemy?" The Stag replied : "Do you only suffer me, friend, to stay where I am, and I will undertake to find some favourable opportunity of effecting my escape." At the approach of the evening the herdsman came to feed his cattle, but did not see the Stag ; and even the farm-bailiff, with several labourers, passed through the shed, and failed to notice him. The Stag, congratulating himself on his safety, began to express his sincere thanks to the Oxen who had kindly afforded him help in the hour of need. One of them again answered him : " We indeed wish you well, but the danger is not over. There is one other yet to pass through the shed, who has as it were a hundred eyes, and until he has come and gone, your life is still in peril." At that moment the master himself entered, and having had to complain that his oxen had not been properly fed, he went up to their racks, and cried out : " Why is there such a scarcity of fodder? There is not half enough straw for them to lie on. Those lazy fellows have not even swept the cobwebs away." While he thus examined everything in turn, he spied the tips of the antlers of the Stag peeping out of the straw. Then summoning his labourers, he ordered that the Stag should be seized, and killed.

THE TWO DOGS.

A MAN had two dogs ; a Hound, trained to assist him in his sports, and a House-dog, taught to watch the house. When he returned home after a good day's sport, he always gave the House-dog a large share of his spoil. The Hound feeling much aggrieved at this, reproached his companion, saying, " It is very hard to have all this labour, while you, who do not assist in the chase, luxuriate on the fruits of my exertions." The House-dog replied, " Do not blame me, my friend, but find fault with the master, who has not taught me to labour, but to depend for subsistence on the labour of others."

Children are not to be blamed for the faults of their parents.

THE WILD ASS AND THE LION.

A WILD Ass and a Lion entered into an alliance, that they might capture the beasts of the forest with the greater ease.   The Lion agreed to assist the Wild Ass with his strength, while the Wild Ass gave the Lion the benefit of his greater speed.   When they had taken as many beasts as their necessities required, the Lion undertook to distribute the prey, and for this purpose divided it into three shares.   " I will take the first share," he said, " because I am King : and the second share, as a partner with you in the chase : and the third share (believe me) will be a source of great evil to you, unless you willingly resign it to me, and set off as fast as you can."

Might makes right.

THE LION AND THE DOLPHIN.

A LION roaming by the sea-shore, saw a Dolphin lift up its head out of the waves, and asked him to contract an alliance with him ; saying that of all the animals they ought to be the best friends, since the one was the king of beasts on the earth, and the other was the sovereign ruler of all the inhabitants of the ocean.   The Dolphin gladly consented to this request.   Not long afterwards the Lion had a combat with a wild bull, and called on the Dolphin to help him.   The Dolphin, though quite willing to give him assistance, was unable to do so, as he could not by any means reach the land.   The Lion abused him as a traitor.   The Dolphin replied, " Nay, my friend, blame not me, but Nature, which, while giving me the sovereignty of the sea, has quite denied me the power of living upon the land."

THE EAGLE AND THE ARROW.

An Eagle sat on a lofty rock, watching the movements of a Hare, whom he sought to make his prey. An archer who saw him from a place of concealment, took an accurate aim, and wounded him mortally. The Eagle gave one look at the arrow that had entered his heart, and saw in that single glance that its feathers had been furnished by himself. "It is a double grief to me," he exclaimed, "that I should perish by an arrow feathered from my own wings."

A consciousness of misfortunes arising from a man's own misconduct aggravates their bitterness.

THE SICK KITE.

A Kite, sick unto death, said to his mother: "O Mother! do not mourn, but at once invoke the gods that my life may be prolonged." She replied, "Alas! my son, which of the gods do you think will pity you? Is there one whom you have not outraged by filching from their very altars a part of the sacrifice offered up to them?"

We must make friends in prosperity, if we would have their help in adversity.

THE LION AND THE BOAR.

On a summer day, when the great heat induced a general thirst, a Lion and a Boar came at the same moment to a small well to drink. They fiercely disputed which of them should drink first, and were soon engaged in the agonies of a mortal combat. On their stopping on a sudden to take breath for the fiercer renewal of the strife, they saw some Vultures waiting in the distance to feast on the one which should fall first. They at once made up their quarrel, saying, "It is better for us to make friends, than to become the food of Crows or Vultures."

THE MICE IN COUNCIL.

The Mice summoned a council to decide how they might best devise means for obtaining notice of the approach of their great enemy the Cat. Among the many plans devised, the one that found most favour was the proposal to tie a bell to the neck of the Cat, that the Mice being warned by the sound of the tinkling might run away and hide themselves in their holes at his approach. But when the Mice further debated who among them should thus "bell the Cat," there was no one found to do it.

THE ONE-EYED DOE.

A Doe, blind of an eye, was accustomed to graze as near to the edge of the cliff as she possibly could, in the hope of securing her greater safety. She turned her sound eye towards the land, that she might get the earliest tidings of the approach of hunter or hound, and her injured eye towards the sea, from whence she entertained no anticipation of danger. Some boatmen sailing by, saw her, and taking a successful aim, mortally wounded her. Yielding up her breath, she gasped forth this lament: "O wretched creature that I am! to take such precaution against the land, and after all to find this sea-shore, to which I had come for safety, so much more perilous."

THE MICE AND THE WEASELS.

The Weasels and the Mice waged a perpetual warfare with each other, in which much blood was shed. The

Weasels were always the victors. The Mice thought
that the cause of their frequent defeats was, that they
had not leaders set apart from the general army to
command them, and that they were exposed to dangers
from want of discipline. They chose therefore such
mice as were most renowned for their family descent,
strength, and counsel, as well as most noted for their
courage in the fight, that they might marshal them in
battle array, and form them into troops, regiments,
and battalions. When all this was done, and the army
disciplined, and the herald Mouse had duly proclaimed
war by challenging the Weasels, the newly chosen
generals bound their heads with straws, that they might
be more conspicuous to all their troops. Scarcely had
the battle commenced, when a great rout overwhelmed
the Mice, who scampered off as fast as they could to
their holes. The generals not being able to get in on
account of the ornaments on their heads, were all captured and eaten by the Weasels.

The more honour the more danger.

THE SHEPHERD AND THE SEA.

A SHEPHERD, keeping watch over his sheep near the
shore, saw the Sea very calm and smooth, and longed
to make a voyage with a view to traffic. He sold all
his flock, and invested it in a cargo of dates and set
sail. But a very great tempest coming on, and the
ship being in danger of sinking, he threw all his mer-
chandise overboard, and hardly escaped with his life
in the empty ship. Not long afterwards, on some one
passing by, and observing the unruffled calm of the sea,
he interrupted him and said, "Belike it is again in want
of dates, and therefore looks quiet."

THE ASS, THE COCK, AND THE LION.

An Ass and a Cock were in a straw-yard together, when a Lion, desperate from hunger, approached the spot. He was about to spring upon the Ass, when the Cock (to the sound of whose voice the Lion, it is said, has a singular aversion) crowed loudly, and the Lion fled away as fast as he could. The Ass observing his trepidation at the mere crowing of a Cock, summoned courage to attack him, and galloped after him for that purpose. He had run no long distance, when the Lion turning about, seized him and tore him to pieces.

False confidence often leads into danger.

THE RIVERS AND THE SEA.

The Rivers joined together to complain to the Sea, saying, "Why is it that when we flow into your tides so potable and sweet, you work in us such a change, and make us salt and unfit to drink?" The Sea, perceiving that they intended to throw the blame on him, said, "Pray cease to flow into me, and then you will not be made briny."

Some find fault with those things by which they are chiefly benefited.

THE WILD BOAR AND THE FOX.

A Wild Boar stood under a tree, and rubbed his tusks against the trunk. A Fox passing by, asked him why he thus sharpened his teeth when there was no danger threatening from either huntsman or hound. He replied, "I do it advisedly; for it would never do to have to sharpen my weapons just at the time I ought to be using them."

To be well prepared for war is the best guarantee of peace.

THE MILKWOMAN AND HER PAIL.

A FARMER'S daughter was carrying her pail of milk from the field to the farm-house, when she fell a-musing. "The money for which this milk will be sold, will buy at least three hundred eggs. The eggs, allowing for all mishaps, will produce two hundred and fifty chickens. The chickens will become ready for the market when poultry will fetch the highest price; so that by the end of the year I shall have money enough from the perquisites that will fall to my share, to buy a new gown. In this dress I will go to the Christmas junketings, when all the young fellows will propose to me, but I will toss my head, and refuse them every one." At this moment she tossed her head in unison with her thoughts, when down fell the Milk-pail to the ground, and all her imaginary schemes perished in a moment.

THE BEE AND JUPITER.

A BEE from Mount Hymettus, the queen of the hive, ascended to Olympus, to present to Jupiter some honey fresh from her combs. Jupiter, delighted with the offering of honey, promised to give whatever she should ask. She therefore besought him saying, "Give me, I pray thee, a sting, that if any mortal shall approach to take my honey, I may kill him." Jupiter was much displeased, for he loved much the race of man; but could not refuse the request on account of his promise. He thus answered the Bee: "You shall have your request; but it will be at the peril of your own life. For if you use your sting, it shall remain in the wound you make, and then you will die from the loss of it."

Evil wishes, like chickens, come home to roost.

THE WOLF AND THE HOUSE-DOG.

A Wolf, meeting with a big well-fed Mastiff having a wooden collar about his neck, inquired of him who it was that fed him so well, and yet compelled him to drag that heavy log about wherever he went. "The master," he replied. Then said the Wolf: "May no friend of mine ever be in such a plight; for the weight of this chain is enough to spoil the appetite."

THE THREE TRADESMEN.

A great city was besieged, and its inhabitants were called together to consider the best means of protecting it from the enemy. A Bricklayer present earnestly recommended bricks, as affording the best materials for an effectual resistance. A Carpenter with equal energy proposed timber, as providing a preferable method of defence. Upon which a Currier stood up, and said, "Sirs, I differ from you altogether: there is no material for resistance equal to a covering of hides; and nothing so good as leather."

Every man for himself.

THE ASS CARRYING THE IMAGE.

An Ass once carried through the streets of a city a famous wooden Image, to be placed in one of its Temples. The crowd as he passed along made lowly prostration before the Image. The Ass, thinking that they bowed their heads in token of respect for himself, bristled up with pride and gave himself airs, and refused to move another step. The driver seeing him thus stop, laid his whip lustily about his shoulders, and said, " O you perverse dull-head ! it is not yet come to this, that men pay worship to an Ass."

They are not wise who take to themselves the credit due to others.

THE MASTER AND HIS DOGS.

A certain man, detained by a storm in his country house, first of all killed his sheep, and then his goats, for the maintenance of his household. The storm still continuing, he was obliged to slaughter his yoke oxen for food. On seeing this, his Dogs took counsel together, and said, " It is time· for us to be off: for if the master spare not his oxen, who work for his gain, how can we expect him to spare us ?"

He is not to be trusted as a friend who illtreats his own family.

THE OLD HOUND.

A Hound, who in the days of his youth and strength had never yielded to any beast of the forest, encountered in his old age a boar in the chase. He seized him boldly by the ear, but could not retain his hold because of the decay of his teeth, so that the boar escaped. His master, quickly coming up, was very much disappointed, and fiercely abused the dog. The Hound looked up, and said, "It was not my fault, master; my spirit was as good as ever, but I could not help mine infirmities. I rather deserve to be praised for what I have been, than to be blamed for what I am."

THE TWO TRAVELLERS AND THE AXE.

Two men were journeying together in each other's company. One of them picked up an axe that lay upon the path, and said, " I have found an axe." " Nay, my friend," replied the other, " do not say ' I,' but ' We' have found an axe." They had not gone far before they saw the owner of the axe pursuing them, when he who had picked up the axe, said, "We are undone." " Nay," replied the other, " keep to your first mode of speech, my friend ; what you thought right then, think right now. Say ' I,' not ' We' are undone."

He who shares the danger ought to share the prize.

THE OLD LION.

A Lion, worn out with years, and powerless from disease, lay on the ground at the point of death. A Boar rushed upon him, and avenged with a stroke of his tusks a long-remembered injury. Shortly afterwards the Bull with his horns gored him as if he were an enemy. When the Ass saw that the huge·beast could be assailed with impunity, he let drive at his forehead with his heels. The expiring Lion said, " I have reluctantly brooked the insults of the brave, but to be compelled to endure contumely from thee, a disgrace to Nature, is indeed to die a double death."

THE WOLF AND THE SHEPHERDS.

A Wolf passing by, saw some Shepherds in a hut eating for their dinner a haunch of mutton. Approaching them, he said, "What a clamour you would raise if I were to do as you are doing !"

THE SEASIDE TRAVELLERS.

SOME travellers, journeying along the sea-shore, climbed to the summit of a tall cliff, and from thence looking over the sea, saw in the distance what they thought was a large ship, and waited in the hope of seeing it enter the harbour. But as the object on which they looked was driven by the wind nearer to the shore, they found that it could at the most be a small boat, and not a ship. When however it reached the beach, they discovered that it was only a large fagot of sticks, and one of them said to his companions, "We have waited for no purpose, for after all there is nothing to see but a fagot."

Our mere anticipations of life outrun its realities.

THE ASS AND HIS SHADOW.

A TRAVELLER hired an Ass to convey him to a distant place. The day being intensely hot, and the sun shining in its strength, the traveller stopped to rest, and sought shelter from the heat under the Shadow of the Ass. As this afforded only protection for one, and as the traveller and the owner of the Ass both claimed it, a violent dispute arose between them as to which of them had the right to it. The owner maintained that he had let the Ass only, and not his Shadow. The traveller asserted that he had, with the hire of the Ass, hired his Shadow also. The quarrel proceeded from words to blows, and while the men fought the Ass galloped off.

In quarrelling about the shadow we often lose the substance.

THE ASS AND HIS MASTERS.

AN Ass belonging to a herb-seller, who gave him too little food and too much work, made a petition to Jupiter that he would release him from his present service, and provide him with another master. Jupiter, after warning him that he would repent his request, caused him to be sold to a tile-maker. Shortly afterwards, finding that he had heavier loads to carry, and harder work in the brick-field, he petitioned for another change of master. Jupiter, telling him that it should be the last time that he could grant his request, ordained that he should be sold to a tanner. The Ass finding that he had fallen into worse hands, and noting his master's occupation, said, groaning: "It would have been better for me to have been either starved by the one, or to have been overworked by the other of my former masters, than to have been bought by my present owner, who will even after I am dead tan my hide, and make me useful to him."

MERCURY AND THE SCULPTOR.

MERCURY once determined to learn in what esteem he was held among mortals. For this purpose he assumed the character of a man, and visited in this disguise a Sculptor's studio. Having looked at various statues, he demanded the price of two figures of Jupiter and of Juno. When the sum at which they were valued was named, he pointed to a figure of himself, saying to the Sculptor, "You will certainly want much more for this, as it is the statue of the Messenger of the Gods, and the author of all your gain." The Sculptor replied, "Well, if you will buy these, I'll fling you that into the bargain."

THE FOX AND THE WOOD-CUTTER.

A Fox running before the hounds, came across a Wood-cutter felling an oak, and besought him to show him a safe hiding-place. The Wood-cutter advised him to take shelter in his own hut. The Fox crept in, and hid himself in a corner. The huntsman came up, with his hounds, in a few minutes, and inquired of the Wood-cutter if he had seen the Fox. He declared that he had not seen him, and yet pointed, all the time he was speaking, to the hut where the Fox lay hid. The huntsman took no notice of the signs, but, believing his word, hastened forward in the chase. As soon as they were well away, the Fox departed without taking any notice of the Wood-cutter: whereon he called to him, and reproached him, saying, "You ungrateful fellow, you owe your life to me, and yet you leave me without a word of thanks." The Fox replied, "Indeed, I should have thanked you fervently, if your deeds had been as good as your words, and if your hands had not been traitors to your speech."

THE OAK AND THE REEDS.

A VERY large Oak was uprooted by the wind, and thrown across a stream. It fell among some Reeds, which it thus addressed: "I wonder how you, who are so light and weak, are not entirely crushed by these strong winds." They replied, "You fight and contend with the wind, and consequently you are destroyed; while we on the contrary bend before the least breath of air, and therefore remain unbroken, and escape."

Stoop to conquer.

THE LION IN A FARMYARD.

A LION entered a farm-yard. The farmer, wishing to catch him, shut the gate. The Lion, when he found that he could not escape, flew upon the sheep, and killed them, and then attacked the oxen. The farmer, beginning to be alarmed for his own safety, opened the gate, when the Lion got off as fast as he could. On his departure the farmer grievously lamented the destruction of his sheep and oxen; when his wife, who had been a spectator of all that took place, said, "On my word, you are rightly served; for how could you for a moment think of shutting up a Lion along with you in the farm-yard, when you know that you shake in your shoes if you only hear his roar at ever so great a distance?"

THE WOLF AND THE LION.

A WOLF having stolen a lamb from a fold, was carrying him off to his lair. A Lion met him in the path, and, seizing the lamb, took it from him. The Wolf, standing at a safe distance, exclaimed, "You have unrighteously taken that which was mine from me." The Lion jeeringly replied, "It was righteously yours, eh? the gift of a friend?"

_____

THE BIRDCATCHER, THE PARTRIDGE, AND THE COCK.

A BIRDCATCHER was about to sit down to a dinner of herbs, when a friend unexpectedly came in. The bird-trap was quite empty, as he had caught nothing. He proceeded to kill a pied Partridge, which he had tamed for a decoy. He entreated thus earnestly for his life: "What would you do without me when next you spread your nets? Who would chirp you to sleep, or call for you the covey of answering birds?" The Birdcatcher spared his life, and determined to pick out a fine young Cock just attaining to his comb. He thus expostulated in piteous tones from his perch: "If you kill me, who will announce to you the appearance of the dawn? Who will wake you to your daily tasks? or tell you when it is time to visit the bird-trap in the morning?" He replied, "What you say is true. You are a capital bird at telling the time of day. But I and the friend who has come in must have our dinners."

Necessity knows no law.

THE ANT AND THE DOVE.

An Ant went to the bank of a river to quench its thirst, and, being carried away by the rush of the stream, was on the point of being drowned. A Dove, sitting on a tree overhanging the water, plucked a leaf, and let it fall into the stream close to her. The Ant, climbing on to it, floated in safety to the bank. Shortly afterwards a birdcatcher came and stood under the tree, and laid his lime-twigs for the Dove, which sat in the branches. The Ant, perceiving his design, stung him in the foot. He suddenly threw down the twigs, and thereupon made the Dove take wing.

The grateful heart will always find opportunities to show its gratitude.

THE HARES AND THE FROGS.

THE Hares, oppressed with a sense of their own exceeding timidity, and weary of the perpetual alarm to which they were exposed, with one accord determined to put an end to themselves and their troubles, by jumping from a lofty precipice into a deep lake below. As they scampered off in a very numerous body to carry out their resolve, the Frogs lying on the banks of the lake heard the noise of their feet, and rushed helter-skelter to the deep water for safety. On seeing the rapid disappearance of the Frogs, one of the Hares cried out to his companions: "Stay, my friends, do not do as you intended; for you now see that other creatures who yet live are more timorous than ourselves."

THE MONKEY AND THE FISHERMEN.

A MONKEY perched upon a lofty tree saw some Fishermen casting their nets into a river, and narrowly watched their proceedings. The Fishermen after a while gave over fishing, and, on going home to dinner, left their nets upon the bank. The Monkey, who is the most imitative of animals, descended from the tree-top, and endeavoured to do as they had done. Having handled the net, he threw it into the river, but became entangled in the meshes. When drowning, he said to himself, " I am rightly served ; for what business had I who had never handled a net to try and catch fish ? "

THE SWAN AND THE GOOSE.

A CERTAIN rich man bought in the market a Goose and a Swan. He fed the one for his table, and kept the other for the sake of its song. When the time came for killing the Goose, the cook went to take him at night, when it was dark, and he was not able to distinguish one bird from the other, and he caught the Swan instead of the Goose. The Swan, threatened with death, burst forth into song, and thus made himself known by his voice, and preserved his life by his melody.

A word in season is most precious.

THE DOE AND THE LION.

A DOE hard pressed by hunters entered a cave for shelter which belonged to a Lion. The Lion concealed himself on seeing her approach; but, when she was safe within the cave, sprang upon her, and tore her to pieces. "Woe is me," exclaimed the Doe, "who have escaped from man, only to throw myself into the mouth of a wild beast!"

In avoiding one evil care must be taken not to fall into another.

_____

THE FISHERMAN AND THE LITTLE FISH.

A FISHERMAN who lived on the produce of his nets, one day caught a single small fish as the result of his day's labour. The fish, panting convulsively, thus entreated for his life: "O Sir, what good can I be to you, and how little am I worth? I am not yet come to my full size. Pray spare my life, and put me back into the sea. I shall soon become a large fish, fit for the tables of the rich; and then you can catch me again, and make a handsome profit of me." The fisherman replied, "I should indeed be a very simple fellow, if, for the chance of a greater uncertain profit, I were to forego my present certain gain."

_____

THE HUNTER AND THE WOODMAN.

A HUNTER, not very bold, was searching for the tracks of a Lion. He asked a man felling oaks in the forest if he had seen any marks of his footsteps, or if he knew where his lair was. "I will," he said, "at once show you the Lion himself." The Hunter, turning very pale, and chattering with his teeth from fear, replied, "No, thank you. I did not ask that; it is his track only I am in search of, not the Lion himself."

The hero is brave in deeds as well as words.

THE SWOLLEN FOX.

A Fox, very much famished, seeing some bread and meat left by shepherds in the hollow of an oak, crept into the hole and made a hearty meal. When he finished, he was so full that he was not able to get out, and began to groan and lament very sadly. Another Fox passing by, heard his cries, and coming up, inquired the cause of his complaining. On learning what had happened, he said to him, " Ah, you will have to remain there, my friend, until you become such as you were when you crept in, and then you will easily get out."

THE TWO FROGS.

Two Frogs dwelt in the same pool. The pool being dried up under the summer's heat, they left it, and set out together for another home. As they went along they chanced to pass a deep well, amply supplied with water, on seeing which one of the Frogs said to the other, " Let us descend and make our abode in this well: it will furnish us with shelter and food." The other replied with greater caution, " But suppose the water should fail us, how can we get out again from so great a depth?"

Do nothing without a regard to the consequences.

THE LAMP.

A Lamp soaked with too much oil, and flaring very much, boasted that it gave more light than the sun. A sudden puff of wind arising, it was immediately extinguished. Its owner lit it again, and said : " Boast no more, but henceforth be content to give thy light in silence. Know that not even the stars need to be relit."

THE CAMEL AND THE ARAB.

An Arab Camel-driver having completed the lading of his Camel, asked him which he would like best, to go up hill or down hill. The poor beast replied, not without a touch of reason: "Why do you ask me? Is it that the level way through the desert is closed?"

THE MILLER, HIS SON, AND THEIR ASS.

A Miller and his son were driving their Ass to a neighbouring fair to sell him. They had not gone far when they met with a troop of women collected round a well, talking and laughing. "Look there," cried one of them, "did you ever see such fellows, to be trudging along the road on foot when they might ride?" The old man hearing this quickly made his son mount the Ass, and continued to walk along merrily by his side. Presently they came up to a group of old men in earnest debate. "There," said one of them, "it proves what I was a-saying. What respect is shown to old age in these days? Do you see that idle lad riding

while his old father has to walk? Get down, you young
scapegrace, and let the old man rest his weary limbs."
Upon this the old man made his son dismount, and
got up himself. In this manner they had not proceeded far when they met a company of women and
children: "Why, you lazy old fellow," cried several
tongues at once, "how can you ride upon the beast,
while that poor little lad there can hardly keep pace
by the side of you?" The good-natured Miller immediately took up his son beside him. They had now
almost reached the town.

"Pray, honest friend," said a citizen, "is that Ass
your own?" "Yes," says the old man. "O, one
would not have thought so," said the other, "by the
way you load him. Why, you two fellows are better
able to carry the poor beast than he you." "Anything
to please you," said the old man; "we can but try."
So, alighting with his son, they tied the legs of the
Ass together, and by the help of a pole endeavoured
to carry him on their shoulders over a bridge near the
entrance of the town. This entertaining sight brought
the people in crowds to laugh at it; till the Ass, not
liking the noise, nor the strange handling that he was
subject to, broke the cords that bound him, and,
tumbling off the pole, fell into the river. Upon this,
the old man, vexed and ashamed, made the best of
his way home again, convinced that by endeavouring
to please everybody he had pleased nobody, and lost
his Ass into the bargain.

THE CAT AND THE MICE.

A CERTAIN house was overrun with Mice. A Cat discovering this, made her way into it, and began to catch and eat them one by one. The Mice being continually devoured, kept themselves close in their holes. The Cat, no longer able to get at them, perceived that she must tempt them forth by some device. For this purpose she jumped upon a peg, and suspending herself from it, pretended to be dead. One of the Mice, peeping stealthily out, saw her, and said, "Ah, my good madam, even though you should turn into a meal-bag, we will not come near you."

THE MOUSE AND THE BULL.

A BULL was bitten by a Mouse, and, pained by the wound, tried to capture him. The Mouse first reached his hole in safety, and the Bull dug into the walls with his horns, until wearied, crouching down, he slept by the hole. The Mouse peeping out, crept furtively up his flank, and, again biting him, retreated to his hole. The Bull rising up, and not knowing what to do, was sadly perplexed. The Mouse murmured forth, " The great do not always prevail. There are times when the small and lowly are the strongest to do mischief."

THE DOG AND THE COOK.

A RICH man gave a great feast, to which he invited many friends and acquaintances. His dog availed himself of the occasion to invite a stranger dog, a friend of his, saying, " My master gives a feast; you will have unusually good cheer; come and sup with me to-night." The Dog thus invited went at the hour appointed, and seeing the preparations for so grand an entertainment, said, in the joy of his heart, " How glad I am that I came! I do not often get such a chance as this. I will take care and eat enough to last me both to-day and to-morrow." While he thus congratulated himself, and wagged his tail, as if he would convey a sense of his pleasure to his friend, the Cook saw him moving about among his dishes, and, seizing him by his fore and hind paws, bundled him without ceremony out of the window. He fell with force upon the ground, and limped away, howling dreadfully. His yelling soon attracted other street dogs, who came up to him, and inquired how he had enjoyed his supper. He replied, "Why, to tell you the truth, I drank so much wine that I remember nothing. I do not know how I got out of the house."

Uninvited guests seldom meet a welcome.

THE THIEVES AND THE COCK.

SOME Thieves broke into a house, and found nothing but a Cock, whom they stole, and got off as fast as they could. On arriving at home they proceeded to kill the Cock, who thus pleaded for his life: "Pray spare. me; I am very serviceable to men. I wake them up in the night to their work." "That is the very reason why we must the more kill you," they replied; "for when you wake your neighbours, you entirely put an end to our business."

The safeguards of virtue are hateful to the evil disposed.

THE DANCING MONKEYS.

A PRINCE had some Monkeys trained to dance. Being naturally great mimics of men's actions, they showed themselves most apt pupils; and, when arrayed in their rich clothes and masks, they danced as well as any of the courtiers. The spectacle was often repeated with great applause, till on one occasion a courtier, bent on mischief, took from his pocket a handful of nuts, and threw them upon the stage. The Monkeys at the sight of the nuts forgot their dancing, and became (as indeed they were) Monkeys instead of actors, and pulling off their masks, and tearing their robes, they fought with one another for the nuts. The dancing spectacle thus came to an end, amidst the laughter and ridicule of the audience.

THE FARMER AND THE FOX.

A FARMER, having a long spite against a Fox for robbing his poultry yard, caught him at last, and, being determined to take an ample revenge, tied some tow well soaked in oil to his tail, and set it on fire. The Fox by a strange fatality rushed to the fields of the Farmer who had captured him. It was the time of the wheat harvest; but the Farmer reaped nothing that year, and returned home grieving sorely.

THE TRAVELLER AND FORTUNE.

A TRAVELLER, wearied with a long journey, lay down overcome with fatigue on the very brink of a deep well. Being within an inch of falling into the water, Dame Fortune, it is said, appeared to him, and waking him from his slumber, thus addressed him: "Good Sir, pray wake up; for had you fallen into the well, the blame will be thrown on me, and I shall get an ill name among mortals; for I find that men are sure to impute their calamities to me, however much by their own folly they have really brought them on themselves."

Every one is more or less master of his own fate.

THE SEA-GULL AND THE KITE.

A SEA-GULL having bolted down too large a fish, burst its deep gullet-bag, and lay down on the shore to die. A Kite seeing him, exclaimed: "You richly deserve your fate; for a bird of the air has no business to seek its food from the sea."

Every man should be content to mind his own business.

THE LION, THE BEAR, AND THE FOX.

A LION and a Bear seized upon a kid at the same moment, and fought fiercely for its possession. When they had fearfully lacerated each other, and were faint from the long combat, they lay down exhausted with fatigue. A Fox, who had gone round them at a distance several times, saw them both stretched on the ground, and the Kid lying untouched in the middle, ran in between them, and seizing the Kid, scampered off as fast as he could. The Lion and the Bear saw him, but not being able to get up, said, " Woe betide us, that we should have fought and belaboured ourselves only to serve the turn of a Fox !"

It sometimes happens that one man has all the toil, and another all the profit.

THE PHILOSOPHER, THE ANTS, AND MERCURY.

A PHILOSOPHER witnessed from the shore the ship-wreck of a vessel, of which the crew and passengers were all drowned. He inveighed against the injustice of Providence, which would for the sake of one criminal perchance sailing in the ship allow so many innocent persons to perish. As he was indulging in these reflections, he found himself surrounded by a whole army of Ants, near to whose nest he was standing. One of them climbed up and stung him, and he immediately trampled them all to death with his foot. Mercury presented himself, and striking the Philosopher with his wand, said, "And are you indeed to make yourself a judge of the dealings of Providence, who hast thyself in a similar manner treated these poor Ants?"

THE PEASANT AND THE EAGLE.

A PEASANT found an Eagle captured in a trap, and, much admiring the bird, set him free. The Eagle did not prove ungrateful to his deliverer, for seeing him sit under a wall, which was not safe, he flew towards him, and snatched off with his talons a bundle resting on his head, and on his rising to pursue him he let the bundle fall again. The Peasant taking it up, and returning to the same place, found the wall under which he had been sitting fallen to the ground; and he much marvelled at the requital made him by the Eagle for the service he had rendered him.

THE FOX AND THE LEOPARD.

THE Fox and the Leopard disputed which was the more beautiful of the two. The Leopard exhibited one by one the various spots which decorated his skin. The Fox, interrupting him, said, "And how much more beautiful than you am I, who am decorated, not in body, but in mind."

THE LION AND THE HARE.

A LION came across a Hare, who was fast asleep on her form. He was just in the act of seizing her, when a fine young Hart trotted by, and he left the Hare to follow him. The Hare, scared by the noise, awoke, and scudded away. The Lion was not able after a long chase to catch the Hart, and returned to feed upon the Hare. On finding that the Hare also had run off, he said, "I am rightly served, for having let go the food that I had in my hand for the chance of obtaining more."

THE IMAGE OF MERCURY AND THE CARPENTER.

A VERY poor man, a Carpenter by trade, had a wooden image of Mercury, before which he made offerings day by day, and entreated the idol to make him rich: but in spite of his entreaties he became poorer and poorer. At last, being very wroth, he took his image down from its pedestal, and dashed it against the wall: when its head being knocked off, out came a stream of gold, which the Carpenter quickly picked up, and said, "Well, I think thou art altogether contradictory and unreasonable; for when I paid you honour, I reaped no benefits: but now that I maltreat you I am loaded with an abundance of riches."

THE LION, THE FOX, AND THE ASS.

THE Lion, the Fox, and the Ass entered into an agreement to assist each other in the chase. Having secured a large booty, the Lion, on their return from the forest, asked the Ass to allot his due portion to each of the three partners in the treaty. The Ass carefully divided the spoil into three equal shares, and modestly requested the two others to make the first choice. The Lion, bursting out into a great rage, devoured the Ass. Then he requested the Fox to do him the favour to make a division. The Fox accumulated all that they had killed into one large heap, and left to himself the smallest possible morsel. The Lion said, "Who has taught you, my very excellent fellow, the art of division? You are perfect to a fraction." He replied, "I learnt it from the Ass, by witnessing his fate."

Happy is the man who learns from the misfortunes of others.

THE BULL AND THE GOAT

A Bull, escaping from a Lion, entered a cave, which some shepherds had lately occupied. A He-goat was left in it, who sharply attacked him with his horns. The Bull quietly addressed him—" Butt away as much as you will. I have no fear of you, but of the Lion. Let that monster once go, and I will soon let you know what is the respective strength of a Goat and a Bull."

It shows an evil disposition to take advantage of a friend in distress.

THE BALD KNIGHT.

A BALD Knight, who wore a wig, went out to hunt. A sudden puff of wind blew off his hat and wig, at which a loud laugh rang forth from his companions. He pulled up his horse, and with great glee joined in the joke by saying, "What marvel that hairs which are not mine should fly from me, when they have forsaken even the man that owns them: with whom, too, they were born!"

THE OAKS AND JUPITER.

THE Oaks presented a complaint to Jupiter, saying, "We bear for no purpose the burden of life, as of all the trees that grow we are the most continually in peril of the axe." Jupiter made answer, "You have only to thank yourselves for the misfortunes to which you are exposed: for if you did not make such excellent pillars and posts, and prove yourselves so serviceable to the carpenters and the farmers, the axe would not so frequently be laid to your roots."

THE MONKEYS AND THEIR MOTHER.

THE Monkey, it is said, has two young ones at a birth. The mother fondles one, and nurtures it with the greatest affection and care; but hates and neglects the other. It happened once on a time that the young one which was caressed and loved was smothered by the too great affection of the mother, while the despised one was nurtured and reared in spite of the neglect to which it was exposed.

The best intentions will not always ensure success.

THE HARE AND THE HOUND.

A HOUND having started a Hare from his form, after a long run, gave up the chase. A Goat-herd seeing him stop, mocked him, saying, "The little one is the best runner of the two." The Hound replied, "You do not see the difference between us: I was only running for a dinner, but he, for his life."

THE SHEPHERD AND THE DOG.

A SHEPHERD penning his sheep in the fold for the night, was about to shut up a wolf with them, when his Dog perceiving the wolf, said, "Master, how can you expect the sheep to be safe if you admit a wolf into the fold?"

THE OAK AND THE WOOD-CUTTERS.

THE Wood-cutters cut down a Mountain Oak, split it in pieces, making wedges of its own branches for dividing the trunk, and for saving their labour. The Oak said with a sigh, "I do not care about the blows of the axe aimed at my roots, but I do grieve at being torn in pieces by these wedges made from my own branches."

Misfortunes springing from ourselves are the hardest to bear.

THE WASP AND THE SNAKE.

A WASP seated himself upon the head of a Snake, and striking him unceasingly with his stings wounded him to death. The Snake, being in great torment, and not knowing how to rid himself of his enemy, or to scare him away, saw a waggon heavily laden with wood, and went and purposely placed his head under the wheels, and said, " I and my enemy shall thus perish together."

THE PEACOCK AND THE CRANE.

A PEACOCK spreading its gorgeous tail mocked a Crane that passed by, ridiculing the ashen hue of its plumage, and saying, "I am robed, like a king, in gold and purple, and all the colours of the rainbow; while you have not a bit of colour on your wings." "True," replied the Crane; "but I soar to the heights of heaven, and lift up my voice to the stars, while you walk below, like a cock, among the birds of the dunghill."

Fine feathers don't make fine birds.

THE HEN AND THE GOLDEN EGGS.

A Cottager and his wife had a Hen, which laid every day a golden egg. They supposed that it must contain a great lump of gold in its inside, and killed it in order that they might get it, when to their surprise they found that the Hen differed in no respect from their other hens. The foolish pair, thus hoping to become rich all at once, deprived themselves of the gain of which they were day by day assured.

THE ASS AND THE FROGS.

An Ass, carrying a load of wood, passed through a pond. As he was crossing through the water he lost his footing, and stumbled and fell, and not being able to rise on account of his load, he groaned heavily. Some Frogs frequenting the pool heard his lamentation, and said, "What would you do if you had to live here always as we do, when you make such a fuss about a mere fall into the water?"

Men often bear little grievances with less courage than they do large misfortunes.

THE CROW AND RAVEN.

A Crow was very jealous of the Raven, because he was considered a bird of good omen, and always attracted the attention of men, as indicating by his flight the good or evil course of future events. Seeing some travellers approaching, she flew up into a tree, and perching herself on one of the branches, cawed as loudly as she could. The travellers turned towards the sound, and wondered what it boded, when one of them said to his companion, "Let us proceed on our journey, my friend, for it is only the caw of a crow, and her cry, you know, is no omen."

Those who assume a character which does not belong to them, only make themselves ridiculous.

THE TREES AND THE AXE.

A MAN came into a forest, and made a petition to the Trees to provide him a handle for his axe. The Trees consented to his request, and gave him a young ash-tree. No sooner had the man fitted from it a new handle to his axe, than he began to use it, and quickly felled with his strokes the noblest giants of the forest. An old oak, lamenting when too late the destruction of his companions, said to a neighbouring cedar, "The first step has lost us all. If we had not given up the rights of the ash, we might yet have retained our own privileges, and have stood for ages."

THE WOLVES AND THE SHEEP-DOGS.

THE Wolves thus addressed the Sheep-dogs: "Why should you, who are like us in so many things, not be entirely of one mind with us, and live with us as brothers should? We differ from you in one point only. We live in freedom, but you bow down to, and slave for, men; who, in return for your services, flog you with whips, and put collars on your necks. They make you also guard their sheep, and while they eat the mutton throw only the bones to you. If you will be persuaded by us, you will give us the sheep, and we will enjoy them in common, till we all are surfeited."

The Dogs listened favourably to these proposals, and, entering the den of the Wolves, they were set upon and torn to pieces.

THE BULL, THE LIONESS, AND THE WILD-BOAR HUNTER.

A BULL finding a lion's cub asleep gored him to death with his horns. The Lioness came up, and bitterly lamented the death of her whelp. A Wild-boar Hunter seeing her distress, stood afar off, and said to her, "Think how many men there are who have reason to lament the loss of their children, whose deaths have been caused by you."

THE BOWMAN AND LION.

A VERY skilful Bowman went to the mountains in search of game. All the beasts of the forest fled at his approach. The Lion alone challenged him to combat. The Bowman immediately let fly an arrow, and said to the Lion: "I send thee my messenger, that from him thou mayest learn what I myself shall be when I assail thee." The Lion, thus wounded, rushed away in great fear, and on a Fox exhorting him to be of good courage, and not to run away at the first attack, he replied: "You counsel me in vain; for if he sends so fearful a messenger, how shall I abide the attack of the man himself?"

A man who can strike from a distance is no pleasant neighbour.

THE CAMEL.

WHEN man first saw the Camel, he was so frightened at his vast size that he fled away. After a time, perceiving the meekness and gentleness of his temper, he summoned courage enough to approach him. Soon afterwards, observing that he was an animal altogether deficient in spirit, he assumed such boldness as to put a bridle in his mouth, and to set a child to drive him.

Use serves to overcome dread.

THE CRAB AND THE FOX.

A CRAB, forsaking the sea-shore, chose a neighbouring green meadow as its feeding ground. A Fox came across him, and being very much famished ate him up. Just as he was on the point of being eaten he said, "I well deserve my fate; for what business had I on the land, when by my nature and habits I am only adapted for the sea?"

Contentment with our lot is an element of happiness.

THE ASS AND THE OLD SHEPHERD.

A SHEPHERD watched his Ass feeding in a meadow. Being alarmed on a sudden by the cries of the enemy, he appealed to the Ass to fly with him, lest they should both be captured. He lazily replied, "Why should I, pray? Do you think it likely the conqueror will place on me two sets of panniers?" "No," rejoined the Shepherd. "Then," said the Ass, "as long as I carry the panniers, what matters it to me whom I serve?"

In a change of government the poor change nothing beyond the name of their master.

THE FOX AND THE HEDGEHOG.

A Fox swimming across a rapid river was carried by the force of the current into a very deep ravine, where he lay for a long time very much bruised and sick, and unable to move. A swarm of hungry blood-sucking flies settled upon him. A Hedgehog passing by compassionated his sufferings, and inquired if he should drive away the flies that were tormenting him. "By no means," replied the Fox; "pray do not molest them." "How is this?" said the Hedgehog; "do you not want to be rid of them?" "No," returned the Fox; "for these flies which you see are full of blood, and sting me but little, and if you rid me of these which are already satiated, others more hungry will come in their place, and will drink up all the blood I have left."

THE WOMAN AND HER HEN.

A WOMAN possessed a Hen that gave her an egg every day. She often thought with herself how she might obtain two eggs daily instead of one, and at last, to gain her purpose, determined to give the Hen a double allowance of barley. From that day the Hen became fat and sleek, and never once laid another egg.

Covetousness overreacheth itself.

THE KITES AND THE SWANS.

THE Kites of old time had, equally with the Swans, the privilege of song. But having heard the neigh of the horse, they were so enchanted with the sound, that they tried to imitate it; and, in trying to neigh, they forgot how to sing.

The desire for imaginary benefits often involves the loss of present blessings.

THE DOG AND THE HARE.

A HOUND having started a Hare on the hill-side, pursued her for some distance: at one time biting her with his teeth as if he would take her life, and at another time fawning upon her, as if in play with another dog. The Hare said to him, " I wish you would act sincerely by me, and show yourself in your true colours. If you are a friend, why do you bite me so hard? if an enemy, why do you fawn on me?"

They are no friends whom you know not whether to trust or to distrust.

THE HARES AND THE FOXES.

THE Hares waged war with the Eagles, and called upon the Foxes to help them. They replied, "We would willingly have helped you, if we had not known who ye were, and with whom ye were fighting."

Count the cost before you commit yourselves.

THE BULL AND THE CALF.

A BULL was striving with all his might to squeeze himself through a narrow passage which led to his stall. A young Calf came up, and offered to go before and show him the way by which he could manage to pass. "Save yourself the trouble," said the Bull; "I knew that way long before you were born."

THE STAG, THE WOLF, AND THE SHEEP.

A STAG asked a Sheep to lend him a measure of wheat, and said that the Wolf would be his surety. The Sheep, fearing some fraud was intended, excused herself, saying, "The Wolf is accustomed to seize what he wants, and to run off; and you, too, can quickly outstrip me in your rapid flight. How then shall I be able to find you, when the day of payment comes?"

Two blacks do not make one white.

THE EAGLE, THE CAT, AND THE WILD SOW.

AN Eagle had made her nest at the top of a lofty oak. A Cat, having found a convenient hole, kittened in the middle of the trunk; and a Wild Sow, with her young, had taken shelter in a hollow at its foot. The Cat resolved to destroy by her arts this chance-made colony.

To carry out her design, she climbed to the nest of the Eagle, and said, "Destruction is preparing for you, and for me too, unfortunately. The Wild Sow, whom you may see daily digging up the earth, wishes to uproot the oak, that she may on its fall seize our families as food for her young." Having thus deprived the Eagle of her senses through terror, she crept down to the cave of the Sow, and said, "Your children are in great danger; for as soon as you shall go out with your litter to find food, the Eagle is prepared to pounce upon one of your little pigs." Having instilled these fears into the Sow, she went and pretended to hide herself in the hollow of the tree. When night came she went forth with silent foot and obtained food for herself and her kittens; but, feigning to be afraid, she kept a look-out all through the day. Meanwhile, the Eagle, full of fear of the Sow, sat still on the branches, and the Sow, terrified by the Eagle, did not dare to go out from her cave; and thus they each, with their families, perished from hunger, and afforded an ample provision to the Cat and her kittens.

————

THE WOLF AND THE FOX.

A very large and strong Wolf was born among the wolves, who exceeded all his fellow-wolves in strength, size, and swiftness, so that they gave him, with unanimous consent, the name of "Lion." The Wolf, with a want of sense proportioned to his enormous size, thought that they gave him this name in earnest, and, leaving his own race, consorted exclusively with the lions. An old sly Fox, seeing this, said, "May I never make myself so ridiculous as you do in your pride and self-conceit; for you really show like a lion among wolves, whereas in a herd of lions you are a wolf."

THE MULE.

A Mule, frolicsome from want of work and from over-much corn, galloped about in a very extravagant manner, and said to himself: "My father surely was a high-mettled racer, and I am his own child in speed and spirit." On the next day, being driven a long journey, and feeling very wearied, he exclaimed in a disconsolate tone: "I must have made a mistake; my father, after all, could have been only an ass."

THE PROPHET.

A Wizard, sitting in the market-place, told the fortunes of the passers-by. A person ran up in great haste, and announced to him that the doors of his house had been broken open, and that all his goods were being stolen. He sighed heavily, and hastened away as fast as he could run. A neighbour saw him running, and said, "Oh! you fellow there! you say you can foretell the fortunes of others; how is it you did not foresee your own?"

THE TWO FROGS.

Two Frogs were neighbours. The one inhabited a deep pond, far removed from public view; the other lived in a gully containing little water, and traversed by a country road. He that lived in the pond warned his friend, and entreated him to change his residence, and to come and live with him, saying that he would enjoy greater safety from danger and more abundant food. The other refused, saying that he felt it so very hard to remove from a place to which he had become accustomed. A few days afterwards a heavy wagon passed through the gully, and crushed him to death under its wheels.

A wilful man will have his way to his own hurt.

THE SERPENT AND THE EAGLE.

A Serpent and an Eagle were struggling with each other in the throes of a deadly conflict. The Serpent had the advantage, and was about to strangle the bird. A countryman saw them, and running up, loosed the coil of the Serpent, and let the Eagle go free. The Serpent, irritated at the escape of his prey, let fly his poison, and injected it into the drinking horn of the countryman. The rustic, ignorant of his danger, was about to drink, when the Eagle struck his hand with his wing, and, seizing the drinking horn in his talons, carried it up aloft.

THE CROW AND THE PITCHER.

A CROW perishing with thirst saw a pitcher, and, hoping to find water, flew to it with great delight. When he reached it, he discovered to his grief that it contained so little water that he could not possibly get at it. He tried everything he could think of to reach the water, but all his efforts were in vain. At last he collected as many stones as he could carry, and dropped them one by one with his beak into the pitcher, until he brought the water within his reach, and thus saved his life.

Necessity is the mother of invention.

THE THIEF AND THE INNKEEPER.

A THIEF hired a room in a tavern, and stayed some days, in the hope of stealing something which should enable him to pay his reckoning. When he had waited some days in vain, he saw the Innkeeper dressed in a new and handsome coat, and sitting before his door. The Thief sat down beside him, and talked with him. As the conversation began to flag, the Thief yawned terribly, and at the same time howled like a wolf. The Innkeeper said, "Why do you howl so fearfully?" "I will tell you," said the Thief: "but first let me ask you to hold my clothes, for I wish to leave them in your hands. I know not, sir, when I got this habit of yawning, nor whether these attacks of howling were inflicted on me as a judgment for my crimes, or for any other cause; but this I do know, that when I yawn for the third time, I actually turn into a wolf, and attack men." With this speech he commenced a second fit of yawning, and again howled as a wolf, as he did at first. The Innkeeper hearing his tale, and, believing what he said, became greatly alarmed, and rising from his seat, attempted to run away. The Thief laid hold of his coat, and entreated him to stop, saying, "Pray wait, sir, and hold my clothes, or I shall tear them to pieces in my fury, when I turn into a wolf." At the same moment he yawned the third time, and set up a howl like a wolf. The Innkeeper, frightened lest he should be attacked, left his new coat in his hand, and ran as fast as he could into the inn for safety. The Thief made off with his new coat, and did not return again to the inn.

Every tale is not to be believed.

THE HART AND THE VINE.

A HART, hard pressed in the chase, hid himself beneath the large leaves of a Vine. The huntsmen, in their haste, overshot the place of his concealment; when the Hart, supposing all danger to have passed, began to nibble the tendrils of the Vine. One of the huntsmen, attracted by the rustling of the leaves, looked back, and, seeing the Hart, shot an arrow from his bow, and killed it. The Hart, at the point of death, groaned out these words, "I am rightly served; for I ought not to have maltreated the Vine that saved me."

THE GNAT AND THE LION.

A GNAT came and said to a Lion, "I do not the least fear you, nor are you stronger than I am. For in what does your strength consist? You can scratch with your claws, and bite with your teeth—so can a woman in her quarrels. I repeat that I am altogether more powerful than you ; and if you doubt it, let us fight and see who will conquer." The Gnat, having sounded his horn, fastened itself upon the Lion, and stung him on the nostrils and the parts of the face devoid of hair. The Lion, trying to crush him, tore himself with his claws, until he punished himself severely. The Gnat thus prevailed over the Lion, and, buzzing about in a song of triumph, flew away. But shortly afterwards he became entangled in the meshes of a cobweb, and was eaten by a spider. He greatly lamented his fate, saying, "Woe is me ! that I, who can wage war successfully with the hugest beasts, should perish myself from this spider, the most inconsiderable of insects !"

THE FOX AND THE GRAPES.

A FAMISHED Fox saw some clusters of ripe black grapes hanging from a trellised vine. She resorted to all her tricks to get at them, but wearied herself in vain, for she could not reach them. At last she turned away, beguiling herself of her disappointment and saying: "The Grapes are sour, and not ripe as I thought."

THE WALNUT-TREE.

A WALNUT-TREE standing by the roadside bore an abundant crop of fruit. The passers-by broke its branches with stones and sticks for the sake of the nuts. The Walnut-tree piteously exclaimed, "O wretched me ! that those whom I cheer with my fruit should repay me with these painful requitals !"

THE KID AND THE WOLF.

A KID, returning without protection from the pasture, was pursued by a Wolf. He turned round, and said to the Wolf: "I know, friend Wolf, that I must be your prey; but before I die, I would ask of you one favour, that you will play me a tune, to which I may dance." The Wolf complied, and while he was piping, and the Kid was dancing, the hounds, hearing the sound, came up, and, issuing forth, gave chase to the Wolf. The Wolf, turning to the Kid, said, "It is just what I deserve; for I, who am only a butcher, should not have turned piper to please you."

THE MONKEY AND THE DOLPHIN.

A SAILOR, bound on a long voyage, took with him a Monkey to amuse him while on shipboard. As he sailed off the coast of Greece, a violent tempest arose, in which the ship was wrecked, and he, his Monkey, and all the crew were obliged to swim for their lives. A Dolphin saw the Monkey contending with the waves, and supposing him to be a man (whom he is always said to befriend), came and placed himself under him, to convey him on his back in safety to the shore. When the Dolphin arrived with his burden in sight of land not far from Athens, he demanded of the Monkey if he were an Athenian, who replied that he was, and that he was descended from one of the most noble families in that city. He then inquired if he knew the Piræus (the famous harbour of Athens). The Monkey, supposing that a man was meant, answered, that he knew him very well, and that he was an intimate friend. The Dolphin, indignant at these falsehoods, dipped the Monkey under the water, and drowned him.

THE HORSE AND THE STAG.

THE Horse had the plain entirely to himself. A Stag intruded into his domain, and shared his pasture. The Horse desiring to revenge himself on the stranger, requested a man, if he were willing, to help him in punishing the Stag. The man replied that, if the Horse would receive a bit in his mouth, and agree to carry him, he would contrive effectual weapons against the Stag. The Horse consented, and allowed the man to mount him. From that hour he found that, instead of obtaining revenge on the Stag, he had enslaved himself to the service of man.

THE JACKDAW AND THE DOVES.

A JACKDAW, seeing some Doves in a cote abundantly provided with food, painting himself white, joined himself to them, that he might share their plentiful maintenance. The Doves as long as he was silent, supposing him to be one of themselves, admitted him to their cote; but when, one day forgetting himself, he began to chatter, they, discovering his true character, drove him forth, pecking him with their beaks. Failing to obtain food among the Doves, he betook himself again to the Jackdaws. They too, not recognizing him on account of his colour, expelled him from living with them. So desiring two objects, he obtained neither.

THE FOX AND THE MONKEY.

A Fox and a Monkey were travelling together on the same road. As they journeyed, they passed through a cemetery full of monuments. "All these monuments which you see," said the Monkey, "are erected in honour of my ancestors, who were in their day freed-men, and citizens of great renown." The Fox replied, "You have chosen a most appropriate subject for your falsehoods, as I am sure none of your ancestors will be able to contradict you."

A false tale often betrays itself.

THE MAN AND HIS WIFE.

A MAN had a Wife who made herself hated by all the members of his household. He wished to find out if she had the same effect on the persons in her father's house. He therefore made some excuse to send her home on a visit to her father. After a short time she returned, when he inquired how she had got on, and how the servants had treated her. She replied, " The neatherds and shepherds cast on me looks of aversion." He said, " O Wife, if you were disliked by those who go out early in the morning with their flocks, and return late in the evening, what must have been felt towards you by those with whom you passed the whole of the day ! "

Straws show how the wind blows.

THE MAN, THE HORSE, THE OX, AND THE DOG.

A Horse, Ox, and Dog, driven to great straits by the cold, sought shelter and protection from Man. He received them kindly, lighted a fire, and warmed them. He made the Horse free of his oats, gave the Ox abundance of hay, and fed the Dog with meat from his own table. Grateful for these favours, they determined to repay him to the best of their ability. They divided for this purpose the term of his life between them, and each endowed one portion of it with the qualities which chiefly characterised himself. The Horse chose his earliest years, and endowed them with his own attributes: hence every man in his youth is impetuous, headstrong, and obstinate in maintaining his own opinion. The Ox took under his patronage the next term of life, and therefore man in his middle age is fond of work, devoted to labour, and resolute to amass wealth, and to husband his resources. The end of life was reserved to the Dog, wherefore the old man is often snappish, irritable, hard to please, and selfish, tolerant only of his own household, but averse to strangers, and to all who do not administer to his comfort or to his necessities.

THE THIEF AND THE HOUSE-DOG.

A THIEF came in the night to break into a house. He brought with him several slices of meat, that he might pacify the House-dog, so that he should not alarm his master by barking. As the Thief threw him the pieces of meat, the Dog said, "If you think to stop my mouth, you will be greatly mistaken. This sudden kindness at your hands will only make me more watchful, lest under these unexpected favours to myself, you have some private ends to accomplish for your own benefit, and for my master's injury."

THE APES AND THE TWO TRAVELLERS.

Two men, one of whom always spoke the truth and the other told nothing but lies, were travelling together, and by chance came to the land of Apes. One of the Apes who had raised himself to be king, commanded them to be laid hold of, and brought before him, that he might know what was said of him among men. He ordered at the same time that all the Apes should be arranged in a long row on his right hand and on his left, and that a throne should be placed for him, as was the custom among men. After these preparations he signified his will that the two men should be brought before him, and greeted them with this salutation : " What sort of a king do I seem to you to be, O strangers ? " The lying Traveller replied, " You seem to me a most mighty king." " And what is your estimate of those you see around me ? " " These," he made answer, " are worthy companions of yourself, fit at least to be ambassadors and leaders of armies." The Ape and all his court, gratified with the lie, commanded a handsome present to be given to the flatterer. On this the truthful Traveller thought within himself, " If so great a reward be given for a lie, with what gift may not I be rewarded, if, according to my custom, I shall tell the truth ? " The Ape quickly turned to him. " And pray how do I and these my friends around me seem to you ? " " Thou art," he said, " a most excellent Ape, and all these thy companions after thy example are excellent Apes too." The King of the Apes, enraged at hearing these truths, gave him over to the teeth and claws of his companions.

THE FOX AND THE LION.

A Fox who had never yet seen a Lion, when he fell in with him by a certain chance for the first time in the forest, was so frightened that he was near dying with fear. On his meeting with him for the second time, he was still much alarmed, but not to the same extent as at first. On seeing him the third time, he so increased in boldness that he went up to him, and commenced a familiar conversation with him.

Acquaintance softens prejudices.

THE WEASEL AND THE MICE.

A Weasel, inactive from age and infirmities, was not able to catch mice as he once did. He therefore rolled himself in flour and lay down in a dark corner. A Mouse, supposing him to be food, leapt upon him, and, being instantly caught, was squeezed to death. Another perished in a similar manner, and then a third, and still others after them. A very old Mouse, who had escaped full many a trap and snare, observing from a safe distance the trick of his crafty foe, said, " Ah ! you that lie there, may you prosper just in the same proportion as you are what you pretend to be !"

THE BOY BATHING.

A Boy bathing in a river was in danger of being drowned. He called out to a traveller, passing by, for help. The traveller, instead of holding out a helping hand, stood by unconcernedly, and scolded the boy for his imprudence. " Oh, sir !" cried the youth, "pray help me now, and scold me afterwards."

Counsel without help, is useless.

THE PEACOCK AND JUNO.

THE Peacock made complaint to Juno that, while the nightingale pleased every ear with his song, he no sooner opened his mouth than he became a laughing-stock to all who heard him. The Goddess, to console him, said, " But you far excel in beauty and in size. The splendour of the emerald shines in your neck, and you unfold a tail gorgeous with painted plumage." " But for what purpose have I," said the bird, " this dumb beauty so long as I am surpassed in song?" " The lot of each," replied Juno, " has been assigned by the will of the Fates—to thee, beauty ; to the eagle, strength ; to the nightingale, song; to the raven, favourable, and to the crow, unfavourable auguries. These are all contented with the endowments allotted to them."

THE WOLF AND THE SHEPHERD.

A WOLF followed a flock of sheep for a long time, and
did not attempt to injure one of them. The Shepherd
at first stood on his guard against him, as against an
enemy, and kept a strict watch over his movements.
But when the Wolf, day after day, kept in the company
of the sheep, and did not make the slightest effort to
seize them, the Shepherd began to look upon him as a
guardian of his flock rather than as a plotter of evil
against it; and when occasion called him one day into
the city, he left the sheep entirely in his charge. The
Wolf, now that he had the opportunity, fell upon the
sheep, and destroyed the greater part of the flock. The
Shepherd on his return, finding his flock destroyed, exclaimed: "I have been rightly served; why did I trust
my sheep to a wolf?"

THE HARES AND THE LIONS.

THE Hares harangued the assembly, and argued that all should be on an equality. The Lions made this reply: "Your words, O Hares! are good; but they lack both claws and teeth such as we have."

THE SELLER OF IMAGES.

A CERTAIN man made a wooden image of Mercury, and offered it for sale. When no one appeared willing to buy it, in order that he might attract purchasers, he cried out that he had the statue to sell of a benefactor, who bestowed wealth and helped to heap up riches. One of the bystanders said to him, "My good fellow, why do you sell him, being such a one as you describe, when you may yourself enjoy the good things he has to give?" "Why," he replied, "I am in want of immediate help, and he is wont to give his good gifts very slowly."

THE HAWK AND THE NIGHTINGALE.

A NIGHTINGALE sitting aloft upon an oak, and singing according to his wont, was seen by a Hawk, who, being in want of food, made a swoop down, and seized him. The Nightingale, about to lose his life, earnestly besought the Hawk to let him go, saying that he was not big enough to satisfy the hunger of a Hawk, who, if he wanted food, ought to pursue the larger birds. The Hawk, interrupting him, said: "I should indeed have lost my senses if I should let go food ready to my hand, for the sake of pursuing birds which are not yet even within sight."

THE LARK AND HER YOUNG ONES.

A LARK had made her nest in the early spring on the young green wheat. The brood had almost grown to their proper strength, and attained the use of their wings and the full plumage of their feathers, when the owner of the field, overlooking his crop, now quite ripe, said, "The time is come when I must send to all my neighbours to help me with my harvest." One of the young Larks heard his speech, and related it to his mother, inquiring of her to what place they should move for safety. "There is no occasion to move yet, my son," she replied; "the man who only sends to his friends to help him with his harvest is not really in earnest." The owner of the field again came a few days later, and saw the wheat shedding the grain from excess of ripeness, and said, "I will come myself to-morrow with my labourers, and with as many reapers as I can hire, and will get in the harvest." The Lark on hearing these words said to her brood, "It is time now to be off, my little ones, for the man is in earnest this time; he no longer trusts to his friends, but will reap the field himself."

Self-help is the best help.

THE DOG, THE COCK, AND THE FOX.

A DOG and a Cock, being great friends, agreed to travel together. At nightfall they took shelter in a thick wood. The Cock, flying up, perched himself on the branches of a tree, while the Dog found a bed beneath in the hollow trunk. When the morning dawned, the Cock, as usual, crowed very loudly several times. A Fox hearing the sound, and wishing to make a breakfast on him, came and stood under the branches, saying how earnestly he desired to make the acquaintance of the owner of so magnificent a voice. The Cock, suspecting his civilities, said: "Sir, I wish you would do me the favour to go round to the hollow trunk below me, and wake up my porter, that he may open the door, and let you in." On the Fox approaching the tree, the Dog sprang out and caught him, and tore him in pieces.

THE GEESE AND THE CRANES.

THE Geese and the Cranes fed in the same meadow. A birdcatcher came to ensnare them in his nets. The Cranes being light of wing, fled away at his approach; while the Geese, being slower of flight and heavier in their bodies, were captured.

THE ASS AND THE WOLF.

An Ass, feeding in a meadow, saw a Wolf approaching to seize him, and immediately pretended to be lame. The Wolf, coming up, inquired the cause of his lameness. The Ass said, that passing through a hedge he trod with his foot upon a sharp thorn, and requested the Wolf to pull it out, lest when he supped on him it should injure his throat. The Wolf consenting, and lifting up the foot, and giving his whole mind to the discovery of the thorn, the Ass with his heels kicked his teeth into his mouth, and galloped away. The Wolf, being thus fearfully mauled, said, "I am rightly served, for why did I attempt the art of healing, when my father only taught me the trade of a butcher?"

THE GOAT AND THE ASS.

A MAN once kept a Goat and an Ass. The Goat envying the Ass on account of his greater abundance of food,
said, "How shamefully you are treated : at one time
grinding in the mill, and at another carrying heavy
burdens;" and he further advised him that he should
pretend to be epileptic, and fall into a ditch and so
obtain rest. The Ass gave credence to his words, and
falling into a ditch, was very much bruised. His master,
sending for a leech, asked his advice. He bade him
pour upon the wounds the lights of a Goat. They at
once killed the Goat, and so healed the Ass.

THE LION AND THE BULL.

A LION, greatly desirous to capture a Bull, and yet
afraid to attack him, on account of his great size, resorted
to a trick to ensure his destruction. He approached
him and said, "I have slain a fine sheep, my friend ;
and if you will come home and partake of him with me,
I shall be delighted to have your company." The Lion
said this in the hope that, as the Bull was in the act of
reclining to eat, he might attack him to advantage, and
make his meal on him. The Bull, however, on his
approach to his den, saw the huge spits and giant cal-
drons, and no sign whatever of the sheep, and, without
saying a word, quietly took his departure. The Lion
inquired why he went off so abruptly, without a word of
salutation to his host, who had not given him any cause
of offence. "I have reasons enough," said the Bull.
"I see no indication whatever of your having slaughtered
a sheep, while I do see, very plainly, every preparation
for your dining on a bull."

THE FOX AND THE MASK.

A Fox entered the house of an actor, and, rummaging through all his properties, came upon a Mask, an admirable imitation of a human head. He placed his paws on it, and said, "What a beautiful head! yet it is of no value, as it entirely wants brains."

THE GRASSHOPPER AND THE OWL.

AN Owl, accustomed to feed at night and to sleep during the day, was greatly disturbed by the noise of a Grasshopper, and earnestly besought her to leave off chirping. The Grasshopper refused to desist, and chirped louder and louder the more the Owl entreated. The Owl, when she saw that she could get no redress, and that her words were despised, attacked the chatterer by a stratagem. "Since I cannot sleep," she said, "on account of your song, which, believe me, is sweet as the lyre of Apollo, I shall indulge myself in drinking some nectar which Pallas lately gave me. If you do not dislike it, come to me, and we will drink it together." The Grasshopper, who was at once thirsty and pleased with the praise of her voice, eagerly flew up. The Owl, coming forth from her hollow, seized her, and put her to death,

THE FOWLER AND THE VIPER.

A FOWLER, taking his bird-lime and his twigs, went out to catch birds. Seeing a thrush sitting upon a tree, he wished to take it, and fitting his twigs to a proper length, he watched intently, having his whole thoughts directed towards the sky. While thus looking upwards, he unawares trod upon a Viper asleep just before his feet. The Viper, turning towards him, stung him; and he, falling into a swoon, said to himself, "Woe is me! that while I proposed to hunt another, am myself fallen unawares into the snares of death."

THE HORSE AND THE ASS.

A HORSE, proud of his fine trappings, met an Ass on the highway. The Ass being heavily laden moved slowly out of the way. "Hardly," said the Horse, "can I resist kicking you with my heels." The Ass held his peace, and made only a silent appeal to the justice of the gods. Not long afterwards the Horse, having become broken-winded, was sent by his owner to the farm. The Ass seeing him drawing a dung-cart, thus derided him: "Where, O boaster, are now all thy gay trappings, thou who art thyself reduced to the condition you so lately treated with contempt?"

THE LION AND THE THREE BULLS.

THREE Bulls for a long time pastured together. A Lion lay in ambush in the hope of making them his prey, but was afraid to attack them whilst they kept together. Having at last by guileful speeches succeeded in separating them, he attacked them without fear, as they fed alone, and feasted on them one by one at his leisure.

Union is strength.

THE WOLF AND THE GOAT.

A WOLF saw a Goat feeding at the summit of a steep precipice, where he had not a chance of reaching her. He called to her and earnestly besought her to come lower down, lest she should by some mishap get a fall; and he added that the meadows lay where he was standing, and that the herbage was most tender. She replied, " No, my friend, it is not me that you invite to the pasture, but you yourself are in want of food."

THE FLY AND THE DRAUGHT-MULE.

A FLY sat on the axle-tree of a chariot, and addressing the Draught-mule said, " How slow you are! Why do you not go faster? See if I do not prick your neck with my sting." The Draught-mule replied, " I do not heed your threats; I only care for him who sits above you, and who quickens my pace with his whip, or holds me back with the reins. Away, therefore, with your insolence, for I know well when to go fast, and when to go slow."

THE FISHERMEN.

SOME Fishermen were out trawling their nets. Perceiving them to be very heavy, they danced about for joy, and supposed that they had taken a large draught of fish. When they had dragged their nets to the shore they found but few fish, and that the nets were full of sand and stones, and they were beyond measure cast down— not so much at the disappointment which had befallen them, as because they had formed such very different expectations. One of their company, an old man, said, " Let us cease lamenting, my mates, for, as it seems to me, sorrow is always the twin sister of joy; and it was only to be looked for that we, who just now were over-rejoiced, should next have something to make us sad."

THE TOWN MOUSE AND THE COUNTRY MOUSE.

A COUNTRY Mouse invited a Town Mouse, an intimate friend, to pay him a visit, and partake of his country fare. As they were on the bare plough-lands, eating their wheat-stalks and roots pulled up from the hedge-row, the Town Mouse said to his friend, "You live here the life of the ants: while in my house is the horn of plenty. I am surrounded with every luxury, and if you will come with me, as I much wish you would, you shall have an ample share of my dainties." The Country Mouse was easily persuaded, and returned to town with his friend. On his arrival the Town Mouse placed before him bread, barley, beans, dried figs, honey, raisins, and, last of all, brought a dainty piece of cheese from a basket. The Country Mouse, being much delighted at the sight of such good cheer. expressed his satisfaction in warm terms, and lamented his own hard fate. Just as they were beginning to eat, some one opened the door, and they both ran off squeaking as fast as they could to a hole so narrow that two could only find room in it by squeezing. They had scarcely again begun their repast when some one else entered to take something out of a cupboard, on which the two Mice, more frightened than before, ran away and hid themselves. At last the Country Mouse, almost famished, thus addressed his friend : " Although you have prepared for me so dainty a feast, I must leave you to enjoy it by yourself. It is surrounded by too many dangers to please me. I prefer my bare plough-lands and roots from the hedge-row, so that I only can live in safety, and without fear."

THE WOLF, THE FOX, AND THE APE.

A WOLF accused a Fox of theft, but he entirely denied the charge. An Ape undertook to adjudge the matter between them. When each had fully stated his case, the Ape pronounced this sentence : " I do not think you, Wolf, ever lost what you claim; and I do believe you, Fox, to have stolen what you so stoutly deny."

The dishonest, if they act honestly, get no credit.

THE WASPS, THE PARTRIDGES, AND THE FARMER.

THE Wasps and the Partridges, overcome with thirst, came to a Farmer and besought him to give them some water to drink. They promised amply to repay him the favour which they asked. The Partridges declared that they would dig around his vines, and make them produce finer grapes. The Wasps said that they would keep guard and drive off thieves with their stings. The Farmer, interrupting them, said: "I have already two oxen, who, without making any promises, do all these things. It is surely better for me to give the water to them than to you."

THE BROTHER AND THE SISTER.

A FATHER had one son and one daughter; the former remarkable for his good looks, the latter for her extraordinary ugliness. While they were playing one day as children, they happened by chance to look together into a mirror that was placed on their mother's chair. The boy congratulated himself on his good looks; the girl grew angry, and could not bear the self-praises of her Brother; interpreting all he said (and how could she do otherwise?) into reflection on herself. She ran off to her father, to be avenged, in her turn, on her Brother, and spitefully accused him of having, as a boy, made use of that which belonged only to girls. The father embraced them both, and bestowing his kisses and affection impartially on each, said: "I wish you both every day to look into the mirror: you, my son, that you may not spoil your beauty by evil conduct; and you, my daughter, that you may make up for your want of beauty by your virtues."

THE DOGS AND THE FOX.

SOME Dogs, finding the skin of a lion, began to tear it in pieces with their teeth. A Fox, seeing them, said, "If this lion were alive, you would soon find out that his claws were stronger than your teeth."

It is easy to kick a man that is down.

THE BLIND MAN AND THE WHELP.

A Blind Man was accustomed to distinguish different animals by touching them with his hands. The whelp of a Wolf was brought him, with a request that he would feel it, and say what it was. He felt it, and being in doubt, said : " I do not quite know whether it is the cub of a Fox, or the whelp of a Wolf; but this I know full well, that it would not be safe to admit him to the sheepfold."

Evil tendencies are shown in early life.

THE COBBLER TURNED DOCTOR.

A Cobbler unable to make a living by his trade, rendered desperate by poverty, began to practise medicine in a town in which he was not known. He sold a drug, pretending that it was an antidote to all poisons, and obtained a great name for himself by long-winded puffs and advertisements. He happened to fall sick himself of a serious illness, on which the Governor of the town determined to test his skill. For this purpose he called for a cup, and while filling it with water, pretended to mix poison with the Cobbler's antidote, and commanded him to drink it, on the promise of a reward. The Cobbler, under the fear of death, confessed that he had no knowledge of medicine, and was only made famous by the stupid clamours of the crowd. The Governor called a public assembly, and thus addressed the citizens: " Of what folly have you been guilty? You have not hesitated to entrust your heads to a man whom no one could employ to make even the shoes for their feet."

THE WOLF AND THE HORSE.

A Wolf coming out of a field of oats met with a Horse, and thus addressed him: "I would advise you to go into that field. It is full of capital oats, which I have left un-touched for you, as you are a friend the very sound of whose teeth it will be a pleasure to me to hear." The Horse replied, "If oats had been the food of wolves, you would never have indulged your ears at the cost of your belly."

Men of evil reputation, when they perform a good deed, fail to get credit for it.

THE TWO MEN WHO WERE ENEMIES.

Two Men, deadly enemies to each other, sailed in the same vessel. Determined to keep as far apart as possible, the one seated himself in the stern, and the other in the prow of the ship. A violent storm having arisen, and the vessel being in great danger of sinking, the one in the stern inquired of the pilot which of the two ends of the ship would go down first. On his replying that he supposed it would be the prow, then said the Man, "Death would not be grievous to me, if I could only see my Enemy die before me."

THE GAME-COCKS AND THE PARTRIDGE.

A Man had two Game-cocks in his poultry-yard. One day by chance he fell in with a tame Partridge for sale. He purchased it, and brought it home that it might be reared with his Game-cocks. On its being put into the poultry-yard they struck at it, and followed it about, so that the Partridge was grievously troubled in mind, and supposed that he was thus evilly treated because he was a stranger. Not long afterwards he saw the Cocks fighting together, and not separating before one had well beaten the other. He then said to himself, "I shall no longer distress myself at being struck at by these Game-cocks, when I see that they cannot even refrain from quarrelling with each other."

THE FOX AND THE LION.

A Fox saw a Lion confined in a cage, and, standing near him, bitterly reviled him. The Lion said to the Fox, "It is not thou who revilest me; but this mischance which has befallen me."

THE QUACK FROG.

A Frog once on a time came forth from his home in the marsh, and made proclamation to all the beasts that he was a learned physician, skilled in the use of drugs, and able to heal all diseases. A Fox asked him, "How can you pretend to prescribe for others, who are unable to heal your own lame gait and wrinkled skin?"

THE LION, THE WOLF, AND THE FOX.

A Lion, growing old, lay sick in his cave. All the beasts came to visit their king, except the Fox. The Wolf, therefore, thinking that he had a capital oppor-

tunity, accused the Fox to the Lion for not paying
any respect to him who had the rule over them all,
and for not coming to visit him. At that very moment
the Fox came in, and heard these last words of the
Wolf. The Lion roaring out in a rage against him, he
sought an opportunity to defend himself, and said,
" And who of all those who have come to you have
benefited you so much as I, who have travelled from
place to place in every direction, and have sought and
learnt from the physicians the means of healing you?"
The Lion commanded him immediately to tell him
the cure, when he replied, "You must flay a wolf alive,
and wrap his skin yet warm around you." The Wolf
was at once taken and flayed; whereon the Fox, turning
to him, said, with a smile, "You should have moved
your master not to ill, but to good, will."

THE DOG'S HOUSE.

A Dog, in the winter time, rolled together and coiled
up in as small a space as possible on account of the
cold, determined to make himself a house. When the
summer returned again he lay asleep, stretched at his
full length, and appeared to himself to be of a great
size, and considered that it would be neither an easy nor
a necessary work to make himself such a house as
would accommodate him.

THE NORTH WIND AND THE SUN.

The North Wind and the Sun disputed which was the
most powerful, and agreed that he should be declared
the victor, who could first strip a wayfaring man of his
clothes. The North Wind first tried his power, and

blew with all his might: but the keener became his blasts, the closer the Traveller wrapped his cloak around him; till at last, resigning all hope of victory, he called upon the Sun to see what he could do. The Sun suddenly shone out with all his warmth. The Traveller no sooner felt his genial rays than he took off one garment after another, and at last, fairly overcome with heat, undressed, and bathed in a stream that lay in his path.

Persuasion is better than Force.

———

THE CROW AND MERCURY.

A CROW caught in a snare prayed to Apollo to release him, making a vow to offer some frankincense at his shrine. Being rescued from his danger, he forgot his promise. Shortly afterwards, on being again caught in a second snare, passing by Apollo he made the same promise to offer frankincense to Mercury, when he appeared, and said to him, "O thou most base fellow! how can I believe thee, who hast disowned and wronged thy former patron?"

———

THE FOX AND THE CRANE.

A Fox invited a Crane to supper, and provided nothing for his entertainment but some soup made of pulse, and poured out into a broad flat stone dish. The soup fell out of the long bill of the Crane at every mouthful, and his vexation at not being able to eat afforded the Fox most intense amusement. The Crane, in his turn, asked the Fox to sup with him, and set before her a flagon, with a long narrow mouth, so that he could easily insert his neck, and enjoy its contents at his leisure; while the Fox, unable even to taste it, met with a fitting requital, after the fashion of her own hospitality.

THE WOLF AND THE LION.

A WOLF, roaming by the mountain side, saw his own shadow, as the sun was setting, become greatly extended and magnified, and he said to himself, " Why should I, being of such an immense size, and extending nearly an acre in length, be afraid of the Lion? Ought I not to be acknowledged as King of all the collected beasts?" While he was indulging in these proud thoughts, a Lion fell upon him, and killed him. He exclaimed with a too late repentance, "Wretched me! this over-estimation of myself is the cause of my destruction."

THE BIRDS, THE BEASTS, AND THE BAT.

THE Birds waged war with the Beasts, and each party were by turns the conquerors. A Bat, fearing the uncertain issues of the fight, always betook himself to that side which was the strongest. When peace was proclaimed, his deceitful conduct was apparent to both the combatants. Therefore being condemned by each for his treachery, he was driven forth from the light of day, and henceforth concealed himself in dark hiding-places, flying always alone and at night.

THE SPENDTHRIFT AND THE SWALLOW.

A YOUNG man, a great spendthrift, had run through all his patrimony, and had but one good cloak left. He happened to see a Swallow, which had appeared before its season, skimming along a pool and twittering gaily. He supposed that summer had come, and went and sold his cloak. Not many days after, the winter having set in again with renewed frost and cold, he found the unfortunate Swallow lifeless on the ground; and said, " Unhappy bird! what have you done? By thus appearing before the spring-time you have not only killed yourself, but you have wrought **my** destruction also."

THE TRUMPETER TAKEN PRISONER.

A TRUMPETER, bravely leading on the soldiers, was captured by the enemy. He cried out to his captors, " Pray spare me, and do not take my life without cause or without inquiry. I have not slain a single man of your troop. I have no arms, and carry nothing but this one brass trumpet." "That is the very reason for which you should be put to death," they said; " for, while you do not fight yourself, your trumpet stirs up all the others to battle."

THE OWL AND THE BIRDS.

AN Owl, in her wisdom, counselled the Birds, when the acorn first began to sprout, to pull it up by all means out of the ground, and not to allow it to grow, because it would produce the mistletoe, from which an irremediable poison, the bird lime, would be extracted, by which they would be captured. The Owl next advised them to pluck up the seed of the flax, which men had sown, as it was a plant which boded no good to them. And, lastly, the Owl, seeing an archer approach, predicted that this man, being on foot, would contrive darts armed with feathers, which should fly faster than the wings of the Birds themselves. The Birds gave no credence to these warning words, but considered the Owl to be beside herself, and said that she was mad. But afterwards, finding her words were true, they wondered at her knowledge, and deemed her to be the wisest of birds. Hence it is that when she appears they resort to her as knowing all things; while she no longer gives them advice, but in solitude laments their past folly.

THE GOODS AND THE ILLS.

ALL the *Goods* were once driven out by the *Ills* from that common share which they each had in the affairs of mankind; for the *Ills* by reason of their numbers had prevailed to possess the earth. The *Goods* wafted themselves to heaven, and asked for a righteous vengeance on their persecutors. They entreated Jupiter that they might no longer be associated with the *Ills*, as they had nothing in common, and could not live together, but were engaged in unceasing warfare, and that an indissoluble law might be laid down, for their future protection. Jupiter granted their request, and decreed that henceforth the *Ills* should visit the earth in company with each other, but that the *Goods* should one by one enter the habitations of men. Hence it arises that *Ills* abound, for they come not one by one, but in troops, and by no means singly: while the *Goods* proceed from Jupiter, and are given, not alike to all, but singly, and separately; and one by one to those who are able to discern them.

THE ASS IN THE LION'S SKIN.

AN ASS, having put on the Lion's skin, roamed about in the forest, and amused himself by frightening all the foolish animals he met with in his wanderings. At last meeting a Fox, he tried to frighten him also, but the Fox no sooner heard the sound of his voice, than he exclaimed, "I might possibly have been frightened myself, if I had not heard your bray."

THE SPARROW AND THE HARE.

A HARE pounced upon by an eagle sobbed very much, and uttered cries like a child. A Sparrow upbraided her, and said, "Where now is thy remarkable swiftness of foot? Why were your feet so slow?" While the Sparrow was thus speaking, a hawk seized him on a sudden, and killed him. The Hare was comforted in her death, and expiring said, " Ah, you who so lately, when you supposed yourself safe, exulted over my calamity, have now yourself reason to deplore a similar misfortune."

THE FLEA AND THE OX.

A FLEA thus questioned the Ox: " What ails you, that, being so huge and strong, you submit to the wrongs you receive from men, and thus slave for them day by day; while I, being so small a creature, mercilessly feed on their flesh, and drink their blood without stint?" The Ox replied: " I do not wish to be ungrateful; for I am loved and well cared for by men, and they often pat my head and shoulders." " Woe's me!" said the Flea; " this very patting which you like, whenever it happens to me, brings with it my inevitable destruction."

THE ASS AND HIS PURCHASER.

A MAN wished to purchase an Ass, and agreed with its owner that he should try him before he bought him. He took the Ass home, and put him in the straw-yard with his other Asses, upon which he left all the others, and joined himself at once to the most idle and the greatest eater of them all. The man put a halter on him, and led him back to his owner; and on his inquiring how, in so short a time, he could have made a trial of him, " I do not need," he answered, "a trial; I know that he will be just such another as the one whom of all the rest he chose for his companion."

A man is known by the company he keeps.

THE DOVE AND THE CROW.

A Dove shut up in a cage was boasting of the large number of the young ones which she had hatched. A Crow hearing her, said: "My good friend, cease from this unseasonable boasting. The larger the number of your family, the greater your cause of sorrow, in seeing them shut up in this prison-house."

THE MAN AND THE SATYR.

A Man and a Satyr once poured out libations together in token of a bond of alliance being formed between them. One very cold wintry day, as they talked together, the Man put his fingers to his mouth and blew on them. On the Satyr inquiring the reason of this, he told him that he did it to warm his hands, they were so cold. Later on in the day they sat down to eat, the food prepared being quite scalding. The Man raised one of the dishes a little towards his mouth and blew in it. On the Satyr again inquiring the reason of this, he said that he did it to cool the meat, it was so hot. "I can no longer consider you as a friend," said the Satyr, "a fellow who with the same breath blows hot and cold."

JUPITER, NEPTUNE, MINERVA, AND MOMUS.

ACCORDING to an ancient legend, the first man was made by Jupiter, the first bull by Neptune, and the first house by Minerva. On the completion of their labours, a dispute arose as to which had made the most perfect work. They agreed to appoint Momus as judge, and to abide by his decision. Momus, however, being very envious of the handicraft of each, found fault with all. He first blamed the work of Neptune, because he had not made the horns of the bull below his eyes, that he might better see where to strike. He then condemned the work of Jupiter, because he had not placed the heart of man on the outside, that everyone might read the thoughts of the evil disposed, and take precautions against the intended mischief. And, lastly, he inveighed against Minerva, because she had not contrived iron wheels in the foundation of her house, that its inhabitants might more easily remove if a neighbour should prove unpleasant. Jupiter, indignant at such inveterate fault-finding, drove him from his office of judge, and expelled him from the mansions of Olympus.

THE EAGLE AND THE JACKDAW.

An Eagle flying down from his eyrie on a lofty rock
seized upon a lamb, and carried him aloft in his talons.
A Jackdaw, who witnessed the capture of the lamb,
was stirred with envy, and determined to emulate the
strength and flight of the Eagle. He flew round with
a great whirr of his wings, and settled upon a large
ram, with the intention of carrying him off, but his
claws becoming entangled in his fleece he was not
able to release himself, although he fluttered with his
feathers as much as he could. The shepherd, seeing
what had happened, ran up and caught him. He at

once clipped his wings, and taking him home at night, gave him to his children. On their saying, " Father, what kind of bird is it?" he replied, " To my certain knowledge he is a Daw; but he will have it that he is an Eagle."

THE EAGLE AND THE FOX.

An Eagle and a Fox formed an intimate friendship, and decided to live near each other. The Eagle built her nest in the branches of a tall tree, while the Fox crept into the underwood and there produced her young. Not long after they had agreed upon this plan, when the Fox was ranging for food, the Eagle, being in want of provision for her young ones, swooped down and seized upon one of the little cubs, and feasted herself and brood. The Fox on her return, discovering what had happened, was less grieved for the death of her young than for her inability to avenge them. A just retribution, however, quickly fell upon the Eagle. While hovering near an altar, on which some villagers were sacrificing a goat, she suddenly seized a piece of the flesh, and carried with it to her nest a burning cinder. A strong breeze soon fanned the spark into a flame, and the eaglets, as yet unfledged and helpless, were roasted in their nest and dropped down dead at the bottom of the tree. The Fox gobbled them up in the sight of the Eagle.

THE TWO BAGS.

Every man, according to an ancient legend, is born into the world with two bags suspended from his neck—a small bag in front full of his neighbours' faults, and a large bag behind filled with his own faults. Hence it is that men are quick to see the faults of others, and yet are often blind to their own failings.

THE BITCH AND HER WHELPS.

A BITCH ready to whelp, earnestly begged of a shepherd a place where she might litter. On her request being granted, she again besought permission to rear her puppies in the same spot. The shepherd again consented. But at last the Bitch, protected with the body-guard of her Whelps, who had now grown up, and were able to defend themselves, asserted her exclusive right to the place, and would not permit the shepherd to approach.

THE STAG AT THE POOL.

A STAG overpowered by heat came to a spring to drink. Seeing his own shadow reflected in the water, he greatly admired the size and variety of his horns, but felt angry with himself for having such slender and weak feet. While he was thus contemplating himself, a Lion appeared at the pool and crouched to spring upon him. The Stag immediately betook himself to flight: and exerting his utmost speed, as long as the plain was smooth and open, kept himself with ease at a safe distance from the Lion. But entering a wood he became entangled by his horns: and the Lion quickly came up with him and caught him. When too late he thus reproached himself: "Woe is me! How have I deceived myself! These feet which would have saved me I despised, and I gloried in these antlers which have proved my destruction."

What is most truly valuable is often underrated.

THE LARK BURYING ITS FATHER.

THE Lark (according to an ancient legend) was created before the earth itself : and when her father died by a fell disease, as there was no earth, she could find for him no place of burial. She let him lie uninterred for five days, and on the sixth day, being in perplexity, she buried him in her own head. Hence she obtained her crest, which is popularly said to be her father's grave-hillock.

Youth's first duty is reverence to parents.

THE GNAT AND THE BULL.

A GNAT settled on the horn of a Bull, and sat there a long time. Just as he was about to fly off, he made a buzzing noise, and inquired of the Bull if he would like him to go. The Bull replied, " I did not know you had come, and I shall not miss you when you go away."

Some men are of more consequence in their own eyes than in the eyes of their neighbours.

THE MONKEY AND THE CAMEL.

THE beasts of the forest gave a splendid entertainment, at which the Monkey stood up and danced. Having vastly delighted the assembly, he sat down amidst universal applause. The Camel, envious of the praises bestowed on the Monkey, and desirous to divert to himself the favour of the guests, proposed to stand up in his turn, and dance for their amusement. He moved about in so utterly ridiculous a manner, that the Beasts in a fit of indignation set upon him with clubs, and drove him out of the assembly.

It is absurd to ape our betters.

THE DOGS AND THE HIDES.

SOME Dogs, famished with hunger, saw some cow-hides steeping in a river. Not being able to reach them, they agreed to drink up the river: but it fell out that they burst themselves with drinking long before they reached the hides.

Attempt not impossibilities.

THE JACKDAW AND THE FOX.

A HALF-FAMISHED Jackdaw seated himself on a fig-tree, which had produced some fruit entirely out of season, and waited in the hope that the figs would ripen. A Fox seeing him sitting so long, and learning the reason of his doing so, said to him, "You are indeed, sir, sadly deceiving yourself; you are indulging a hope strong enough to cheat you, but which will never reward you with enjoyment."

MERCURY AND THE WORKMEN.

A WORKMAN, felling wood by the side of a river, let his axe drop by accident into a deep pool. Being thus deprived of the means of his livelihood, he sat down on the bank, and lamented his hard fate. Mercury appeared, and demanded the cause of his tears. He told him his misfortune, when Mercury plunged into the stream, and, bringing up a golden axe, inquired if that were the one he had lost. On his saying that it was not his, Mercury disappeared beneath the water a second time, and returned with a silver axe in his hand, and again demanded of the Workman " if it were his." On the Workman saying it was not, he dived into the pool for the third time, and brought up the axe that had been lost. On the Workman claiming it, and expressing his joy at its recovery, Mercury, pleased with his honesty, gave him the golden and the silver axes in addition to his own.

The Workman, on his return to his house, related to his companions all that had happened. One of them at once resolved to try whether he could not also secure the same good fortune to himself. He ran to the river, and threw his axe on purpose into the pool at the same place, and sat down on the bank to weep. Mercury appeared to him just as he hoped he would; and having learned the cause of his grief, plunged into the stream, and brought up a golden axe, and inquired if he had lost it. The Workman seized it greedily, and declared that of a truth it was the very same axe that he had lost. Mercury, displeased at his knavery, not only took away the golden axe, but refused to recover for him the axe he had thrown into the pool.

THE PEASANT AND THE APPLE-TREE.

A PEASANT had in his garden an Apple-tree, which bore no fruit, but only served as a harbour for the sparrows and grasshoppers. He resolved to cut it down, and, taking his axe in his hand, made a bold stroke at its roots. The grasshoppers and sparrows entreated him not to cut down the tree that sheltered them, but to spare it, and they would sing to him and lighten his labours. He paid no attention to their request, but gave the tree a second and a third blow with his axe: when he reached the hollow of the tree, he found a hive full of honey. Having tasted the honeycomb, he threw down his axe, and, looking on the tree as sacred, took great care of it.

Self interest alone moves some men.

THE TWO SOLDIERS AND THE ROBBER.

Two Soldiers travelling together, were set upon by a Robber. The one fled away; the other stood his ground, and defended himself with his stout right hand. The Robber being slain, the timid companion runs up and draws his sword, and then, throwing back his travelling cloak, says, "I'll at him, and I'll take care he shall learn whom he has attacked." On this he who had fought with the Robber made answer, "I only wish that you had helped me just now, even if it had been only with those words, for I should have been the more encouraged, believing them to be true; but now put up your sword in its sheath and hold your equally useless tongue, till you can deceive others who do not know you. I, indeed, who have experienced with what speed you run away, know right well that no dependence can be placed on your valour."

THE SHEPHERD AND THE SHEEP.

A SHEPHERD driving his Sheep to a wood, saw an oak of unusual size, full of acorns, and, spreading his cloak under the branches, he climbed up into the tree, and shook down the acorns. The Sheep eating the acorns, inadvertently frayed and tore the cloak. The Shepherd coming down, and seeing what was done, said, "O you most ungrateful creatures! you provide wool to make garments for all other men, but you destroy the clothes of him who feeds you.

THE TREES UNDER THE PROTECTION OF THE GODS.

THE Gods, according to an ancient legend, made choice of certain trees to be under their special protection. Jupiter chose the oak, Venus the myrtle, Apollo the laurel, Cybele the pine, and Hercules the poplar. Minerva, wondering why they had preferred trees not yielding fruit, inquired the reason of their choice. Jupiter replied, "It is lest we should seem to covet the honour for the fruit." But said Minerva, "Let any one say what he will, the olive is more dear to me on account of its fruit." Then said Jupiter, "My daughter, you are rightly called wise; for unless what we do is useful, the glory of it is vain."

THE FLEA AND THE WRESTLER.

A FLEA settled upon the bare foot of a Wrestler, and bit him; on which he called loudly upon Hercules for help. The Flea a second time hopped upon his foot, when he groaned and said, "O Hercules! if you will not help me against a Flea, how can I hope for your assistance against greater antagonists?"

THE LION AND THE FOX.

A Fox entered into partnership with a Lion, on the pretence of becoming his servant. Each undertook his proper duty in accordance with his own nature and powers. The Fox discovered and pointed out the prey, the Lion sprung on it, and seized it. The Fox soon became jealous of the Lion carrying off the Lion's share, and said that he would no longer find out the prey, but would capture it on his own account. The next day he attempted to snatch a lamb from the fold, but fell himself a prey to the huntsmen and hounds.

TRUTH AND THE TRAVELLER.

A WAYFARING Man, travelling in the desert, met a woman standing alone and terribly dejected. He inquired of her, "Who art thou?" "My name is Truth," she replied. "And for what cause," he asked, "have you left the city, to dwell alone here in the wilderness?" She made answer, "Because in former times falsehood was with few, but is now with all men, whether you would hear or speak."

THE MANSLAYER.

A MAN committed a murder, and was pursued by the relations of the man whom he murdered. On his reaching the river Nile he saw a Lion on its bank, and being fearfully afraid, climbed up a tree. He found a serpent in the upper branches of the tree, and again being greatly alarmed, he threw himself into the river, when a crocodile caught him and ate him. Thus the earth, the air, and the water, alike refused shelter to a murderer.

THE LION AND THE EAGLE.

AN Eagle stayed his flight, and entreated a Lion to make an alliance with him to their mutual advantage. The Lion replied, "I have no objection, but you must excuse me for requiring you to find surety for your good faith; for how can I trust any one as a friend, who is able to fly away from his bargain whenever he pleases?"

Try before you trust.

THE ASS AND HIS DRIVER.

An Ass being driven along the high road, suddenly started off, and bolted to the brink of a deep precipice. When he was in the act of throwing himself over, his owner, seizing him by the tail, endeavoured to pull him back. The Ass, persisting in his effort, the man let him go and said, "Conquer: but conquer to your cost."

THE THRUSH AND THE FOWLER.

A Thrush was feeding on a myrtle-tree, and did not move from it, on account of the deliciousness of its berries. A Fowler observing her staying so long in one spot, having well birdlimed his reeds, caught her. The Thrush, being at the point of death, exclaimed, "O foolish creature that I am! For the sake of a little pleasant food I have deprived myself of my life."

THE MOTHER AND THE WOLF.

A famished Wolf was prowling about in the morning in search of food. As he passed the door of a cottage built in the forest, he heard a Mother say to her child, "Be quiet, or I will throw you out of the window, and the Wolf shall eat you." The Wolf sat all day waiting at the door. In the evening he heard the same woman, fondling her child and saying: "He is quiet now, and if the Wolf should come, we will kill him." The Wolf, hearing these words, went home, gaping with cold and hunger. On his reaching his den, Mistress Wolf inquired of him why he returned wearied and supperless, so contrary to his wont. He replied: "Why, forsooth! —because I gave credence to the words of a woman!"

THE HEN AND THE SWALLOW.

A Hen finding the eggs of a viper, and carefully keeping them warm, nourished them into life. A Swallow observing what she had done, said, "You silly creature! why have you hatched these vipers, which, when they shall have grown, will inflict injury on all, beginning with yourself?"

THE ROSE AND THE AMARANTH.

An Amaranth planted in a garden near a Rose-tree thus addressed it: "What a lovely flower is the Rose, a favourite alike with Gods and with men. I envy you your beauty and your perfume." The Rose replied, "I indeed, dear Amaranth, flourish but for a brief season! If no cruel hand pluck me from my stem, yet I must perish by an early doom. But thou art *immortal*, and dost never fade, but bloomest for ever in renewed youth."

THE TRAVELLERS AND THE PLANE-TREE.

Two Travellers, worn out by the heat of the summer's sun, laid themselves down at noon under the wide-spreading branches of a Plane-tree. As they rested under its shade, one of the Travellers said to the other, "What a singularly useless tree is the Plane! It bears no fruit, and is not of the least service to man." The Plane-tree, interrupting him, said, "You ungrateful fellows! Do you, while receiving benefits from me, and resting under my shade, dare to describe me as useless, and unprofitable?"

Some men despise their best blessings.

THE ASS AND THE HORSE.

An Ass besought a Horse to spare him a small portion of his feed. "Yes," said he; "if any remains out of what I am now eating I will give it you, for the sake of my own superior dignity; and if you will come when I shall reach my own stall in the evening, I will give you a little sack full of barley." The Ass replied: "Thank you. I can't think that you, who refuse me a little matter now, will by and by confer on me a greater benefit."

THE CROW AND THE SHEEP.

A troublesome Crow seated herself on the back of a Sheep. The Sheep, much against his will, carried her backward and forward for a long time, and at last said, "If you had treated a dog in this way, you would have had your deserts from his sharp teeth." To this the Crow replied, "I despise the weak, and yield to the strong. I know whom I may bully, and whom I must flatter; and I thus prolong my life to a good old age."

THE FOX AND THE BRAMBLE.

A Fox, mounting a hedge, when he was about to fall caught hold of a Bramble. Having pricked and grievously torn the soles of his feet, he accused the Bramble, because, when he had fled to her for assistance, she had used him worse than the hedge itself. The Bramble, interrupting him, said, "But you really must have been out of your senses to fasten yourself on me, who am myself always accustomed to fasten upon others."

THE ASS AND THE CHARGER.

An Ass congratulated a Horse on being so ungrudgingly and carefully provided for, while he himself had scarcely enough to eat, nor even that without hard work. But when war broke out, and the heavy armed soldier mounted the Horse, and riding him to the charge, rushed into the very midst of the enemy, and the Horse, being wounded, fell dead on the battle-field; then the Ass, seeing all these things, changed his mind, and commiserated the Horse.

THE LION, JUPITER, AND THE ELEPHANT.

The Lion wearied Jupiter with his frequent complaints. "It is true," he said, "O Jupiter! that I am gigantic in strength, handsome in shape, and powerful in attack. I have jaws well provided with teeth, and feet furnished with claws, and I lord it over all the beasts of the forest; and what a disgrace it is, that being such as I am, I should be frightened by the crowing of a cock." Jupiter replied, "Why do you blame me without a cause? I have given you all the attributes which I possess myself, and your courage never fails you except in this one instance." On this the Lion groaned and lamented very much, and reproached himself with his cowardice, and wished that he might die. As these thoughts passed through his mind, he met an Elephant, and came near to hold a conversation with him. After a time he observed that the Elephant shook his ears very often, and he inquired what was the matter, and why his ears moved with such a tremor every now and then. Just at that moment a Gnat settled on the head of the Elephant, and he replied, "Do you see that little buzzing insect? If it enters my ear, my fate is sealed. I should die presently." The Lion said, "Well, since so huge a beast is afraid of a tiny gnat, I will no more complain, nor wish myself dead. I find myself, even as I am, better off than the Elephant, in that very same degree that a Cock is greater than a Gnat."

THE DOG AND THE OYSTER.

A Dog, used to eating eggs, saw an Oyster; and opening his mouth to its widest extent, swallowed it down with the utmost relish, supposing it to be an egg. Soon afterwards suffering great pain in his stomach, he said, "I deserve all this torment, for my folly in thinking that everything round must be an egg."

They who act without sufficient thought will often fall into unsuspected danger.

THE MULES AND THE ROBBERS.

Two Mules well laden with packs were trudging along. One carried panniers filled with money, the other sacks weighted with grain. The Mule carrying the treasure walked with head erect, as if conscious of the value of his burden, and tossed up and down the clear toned bells fastened to his neck. His companion followed with quiet and easy step. All on a sudden Robbers rushed from their hiding-places upon them, and in the scuffle with their owners, wounded with a sword the Mule carrying the treasure, which they greedily seized upon, while they took no notice of the grain. The Mule which had been robbed and wounded, bewailed his misfortunes. The other replied, " I am indeed glad that I was thought so little of, for I have lost nothing, nor am I hurt with any wound."

THE LAMB AND THE WOLF.

A Wolf pursued a Lamb, which fled for refuge to a certain Temple. The Wolf called out to him and said, " The Priest will slay you in sacrifice, if he should catch you," on which the Lamb replied, " It would be better for me to be sacrificed in the Temple, than to be eaten by you."

THE PARTRIDGE AND THE FOWLER.

A Fowler caught a Partridge, and was about to kill it. The Partridge earnestly besought him to spare his life, saying, " Pray, master, permit me to live, and I will entice many Partridges to you in recompense for your mercy to me." The Fowler replied, " I shall now with the less scruple take your life: because you are willing to save it at the cost of betraying your friends and relations."

_____

THE FLEA AND THE MAN.

A MAN, very much annoyed with a Flea, caught him at last, and said, "Who are you who dare to feed on my limbs, and to cost me so much trouble in catching you?" The Flea replied, "O my dear sir, pray spare my life, and destroy me not, for I cannot possibly do you much harm." The Man, laughing, replied, "Now you shall certainly die by mine own hands, for no evil, whether it be small or large, ought to be tolerated."

_____

THE RICH MAN AND THE TANNER.

A RICH man lived near a Tanner, and not being able to bear the unpleasant smell of the tan-yard, he pressed his neighbour to go away. The Tanner put off his departure from time to time, saying that he would remove soon. But as he still continued to stay, it came to pass, as time went on, the rich man became accustomed to the smell, and feeling no manner of inconvenience, made no further complaints.

_____

THE VIPER AND THE FILE.

A VIPER entering the workshop of a smith, sought from the tools the means of satisfying his hunger. He more particularly addressed himself to a File, and asked of him the favour of a meal. The File replied, "You must indeed be a simple-minded fellow if you expect to get anything from me, who am accustomed to take from every one, and never to give anything in return."

The covetous are poor givers.

THE LION AND THE SHEPHERD.

A LION, roaming through a forest, trod upon a thorn, and soon after came up towards a Shepherd, and fawned upon him, wagging his tail, as if he would say, " I am a suppliant, and seek your aid." The Shepherd boldly examined, and discovered the thorn, and placing his foot upon his lap, pulled it out and relieved the Lion of his pain, who returned into the forest. Some time after, the Shepherd being imprisoned on a false accusation, is condemned " to be cast to the Lions," as the punishment of his imputed crime. The Lion, on being released from his cage, recognizes the Shepherd as the man who healed him, and, instead of attacking him, approaches and places his foot upon his lap. The King, as soon as he heard the tale, ordered the Lion to be set free again in the forest, and the Shepherd to be pardoned and restored to his friends.

THE CAMEL AND JUPITER.

THE Camel, when he saw the Bull adorned with horns, envied him, and wished that he himself could obtain the same honours. He went to Jupiter, and besought him to give him horns. Jupiter, vexed at his request, because he was not satisfied with his size and strength of body, and desired yet more, not only refused to give him horns, but even deprived him of a portion of his ears.

THE PANTHER AND THE SHEPHERDS.

A PANTHER, by some mischance, fell into a pit. The Shepherds discovered him, and threw sticks at him, and pelted him with stones, while some of them, moved with compassion towards one about to die even though no one should hurt him, threw in some food to prolong his life. At night they returned home, not dreaming of any danger, but supposing that on the morrow they should find him dead. The Panther, however, when he had recruited his feeble strength, freed himself with a sudden bound from the pit, and hastened home with rapid steps to his den. After a few days he came forth and slaughtered the cattle, and, killing the Shepherds who had attacked him, raged with angry fury. Then they who had spared his life, fearing for their safety, surrendered to him their flocks, and begged only for their lives; to whom the Panther made this reply: "I remember alike those who sought my life with stones, and those who gave me food—lay aside, therefore, your fears. I return as an enemy only to those who injured me."

THE EAGLE AND THE KITE.

An Eagle, overwhelmed with sorrow, sat upon the branches of a tree, in company with a Kite. "Why," said the Kite, "do I see you with such a rueful look?" "I seek," she replied, "for a mate suitable for me, and am not able to find one." "Take me," returned the Kite; "I am much stronger than you are." "Why, are you able to secure the means of living by your plunder?" "Well, I have often caught and carried away an ostrich in my talons." The Eagle, persuaded by these words, accepted him as her mate. Shortly after the nuptials, the Eagle said, "Fly off, and bring me back the ostrich you promised me." The Kite, soaring aloft into the air, brought back the shabbiest possible mouse, and stinking from the length of time it had lain about the

fields. " Is this," said the Eagle, " the faithful fulfilment
of your promise to me ?" The Kite replied, " That I
might attain to your royal hand, there is nothing that I
would not have promised, however much I knew that I
must fail in the performance."

THE EAGLE AND HIS CAPTOR.

AN Eagle was once captured by a man, who at once
clipped his wings, and put him into his poultry yard
with the other birds ; at which treatment the Eagle was
weighed down with grief. Another neighbour having
purchased him, suffered his feathers to grow again.
The Eagle took flight, and pouncing upon a hare
brought it at once as an offering to his benefactor. A
Fox, seeing this, exclaimed, " Do not propitiate the
favour of this man, but of your former owner, lest he
should again hunt for you, and deprive you a second
time of your wings."

THE KING'S SON AND THE PAINTED LION.

A KING who had one only son, fond of martial exer-
cises, had a dream in which he was warned that
his son would be killed by a lion. Afraid lest the
dream should prove true, he built for his son a pleasant
palace, and adorned its walls for his amusement with
all kinds of animals of the size of life, among which
was the picture of a lion. When the young Prince
saw this, his grief at being thus confined burst out
afresh, and, standing near the lion, he thus spoke :
" O you most detestable of animals ? through a lying
dream of my father's, which he saw in his sleep, I am
shut up on your account in this palace as if I had

been a girl: what shall I now do to you?" With these words he stretched out his hands toward a thorn-tree, meaning to cut a stick from its branches that he might beat the lion, when one of its sharp prickles pierced his finger, and caused great pain and inflammation, so that the young Prince fell down in a fainting fit. A violent fever suddenly set in, from which he died not many days after.

We had better bear our troubles bravely than try to escape them.

THE CAT AND VENUS.

A Cat fell in love with a handsome young man, and entreated Venus that she would change her into the form of a woman. Venus consented to her request, and transformed her into a beautiful damsel, so that the youth saw her, and loved her, and took her home as his bride. While they were reclining in their chamber, Venus, wishing to discover if the Cat in her change of shape had also altered her habits of life, let down a mouse in the middle of the room. She, quite forgetting her present condition, started up from the couch, and pursued the mouse, wishing to eat it. Venus, much disappointed, again caused her to return to her former shape.

Nature exceeds nurture.

THE EAGLE AND THE BEETLE.

The Eagle and the Beetle were at enmity together, and they destroyed one another's nests. The Eagle gave the first provocation in seizing upon and in eating the young ones of the Beetle. The Beetle got by stealth at the Eagle's eggs, and rolled them out of the nest, and followed the Eagle even into the presence of Jupiter. On the Eagle making his complaint, Jupiter ordered him to make his nest in his lap; and while Jupiter had the eggs in his lap, the Beetle came flying about him, and Jupiter rising up unawares, to drive him away from his head, threw down the eggs, and broke them.

The weak often revenge themselves on those who use them ill, even though they be the more powerful.

THE SHE-GOATS AND THEIR BEARDS.

THE She-goats having obtained by request from Jupiter the favour of a beard, the He-goats, sorely displeased, made complaint that the females equalled them in dignity. "Suffer them," said Jupiter, "to enjoy an empty honour, and to assume the badge of your nobler sex, so long as they are not your equals in strength or courage."

It matters little if those who are inferior to us in merit should be like us in outside appearances.

THE BALD MAN AND THE FLY.

A FLY bit the bare head of a Bald Man, who, endeavouring to destroy it, gave himself a heavy slap. Then said the Fly mockingly, "You who have wished to revenge, even with death, the prick of a tiny insect, what will you do to yourself, who have added insult to injury?" The Bald Man replied, "I can easily make peace with myself, because I know there was no intention to hurt. But you, an ill-favoured and contemptible insect, who delight in sucking human blood, I wish that I could have killed **you**, even if I had incurred a heavier penalty."

THE SHIPWRECKED MAN AND THE SEA.

A SHIPWRECKED Man, having been cast upon a certain shore, slept after his buffetings with the deep. After a while waking up, when he looked upon the sea, he loaded it with reproaches that, enticing men with the calmness of its looks, when it had induced them to plough its waters, it grew rough and destroyed them utterly. The Sea, assuming the form of a woman, replied to him : "Blame not me, my good sir, but the winds, for I am by my own nature as calm and firm even as this earth; but the winds falling on me on a sudden, create these waves, and lash me into fury."

THE BUFFOON AND THE COUNTRYMAN.

A RICH nobleman once opened the theatres without charge to the people, and gave a public notice that he would handsomely reward any person who should invent a new amusement for the occasion. Various public performers contended for the prize. Among them came a Buffoon well known among the populace for his jokes, and said that he had a kind of entertainment which had never been brought out on any stage before. This report being spread about made a great stir in the place, and the theatre was crowded in every part. The Buffoon appeared alone upon the boards, without any apparatus or confederates, and the very sense of expectation caused an intense silence. The Buffoon suddenly bent his head towards his bosom and imitated the squeaking of a little pig so admirably with his voice that the audience declared that he had a porker under his cloak, and demanded that it should be shaken out. When that was done, and yet nothing was found, they cheered the actor, and loaded him with the loudest applause. A Countryman in the crowd, observing all that had passed, said, "So help me, Hercules, he shall not beat me at that trick!" and at once proclaimed that he would do the same thing on the next day, though in a much more natural way. On the morrow a still larger crowd assembled in the theatre; but now partiality for their favourite actor very generally prevailed, and the audience came rather to ridicule the Countryman than to see the spectacle. Both of the performers, however, appeared on the stage. The Buffoon grunted and squeaked away first, and obtained, as on the preceding day, the applause and cheers of the spectators. Next the Countryman commenced, and pretending that he concealed a little pig beneath his clothes (which in truth he did, but not suspected of the audience), contrived to lay hold of and to pull his ear, when he began to squeak, and to express in his pain the actual cry of the pig. The crowd, however, cried out with one consent that the Buffoon had given a far more exact imitation, and clamoured for the Countryman to be kicked out of the theatre. On this the rustic produced the little pig from his cloak, and showed by the most positive proof the greatness of their mistake. "Look here," he said, "this shows what sort of judges you are."

THE CROW AND THE SERPENT.

A Crow, in great want of food, saw a Serpent asleep in a sunny nook, and flying down, greedily seized him. The Serpent turning about, bit the Crow with a mortal wound; the Crow in the agony of death exclaimed: " O unhappy me ! who have found in that which I deemed a happy windfall the source of my destruction."

THE HUNTER AND THE HORSEMAN

A certain Hunter having snared a hare, placed it upon his shoulders, and set out homewards. He met on his way with a man on horseback who begged the hare of him, under the pretence of purchasing it. The Horseman having got the hare, rode off as fast as he could. The Hunter ran after him, as if he was sure of overtaking him. The Horseman, however, increasing more and more the distance between them, the Hunter, sorely against his will, called out to him, and said, " Get along with you ! for I will now make you a present of the hare."

THE OLIVE-TREE AND THE FIG-TREE.

The Olive-tree ridiculed the Fig-tree because, while she was green all the year round, the Fig-tree changed its leaves with the seasons. A shower of snow fell upon them, and, finding the Olive full of foliage, it settled upon its branches, and, breaking them down with its weight, at once despoiled it of its beauty and killed the tree ; but finding the Fig-tree denuded of leaves, it fell through to the ground, and did not injure it at all.

THE FROGS' COMPLAINT AGAINST THE SUN.

ONCE upon a time, when the Sun announced his intention to take a wife, the Frogs lifted up their voices in
clamour to the sky. Jupiter, disturbed by the noise of
their croaking, inquired the cause of their complaint.
One of them said, "The Sun, now while he is single,
parches up the marsh, and compels us to die miserably
in our arid homes; what will be our future condition if
he should beget other suns?"

THE BRAZIER AND HIS DOG.

A BRAZIER had a little Dog, which was a great favourite
with his master, and his constant companion. While he
hammered away at his metals, the Dog slept; but when,
on the other hand, he went to dinner, and began to eat,
the Dog woke up, and wagged his tail, as if he would
ask for a share of his meal. His master one day, pretending to be angry, and shaking his stick at him, said,
"You wretched little sluggard! what shall I do to you?
While I am hammering on the anvil, you sleep on the
mat; and when I begin to eat after my toil, you wake
up, and wag your tail for food. Do you not know that
labour is the source of every blessing, and that none
but those who work are entitled to eat?"

INDEX.

Made in the USA
Monee, IL
25 February 2021